THE NON-PROPHET'S GUIDE TO THE BOOK OF DANIEL

THE NON-PROPHET'S GUIDE TO THE BOOK OF DANIEL

Written & Illustrated by
TODD HAMPSON

HARVEST PROPHECY
AN IMPRINT OF HARVEST HOUSE PUBLISHERS

Published in association with William K. Jensen Literary Agency, 119 Bampton Court, Eugene, Oregon 97404.

Cover design by Kyler Dougherty

Cover illustration © Todd Hampson

Interior design by Chad Dougherty

For bulk, special sales, or ministry purchases, please call 1-800-547-8979.
Email: Customerservice@hhpbooks.com

This logo is a federally registered trademark of the Hawkins Children's LLC. Harvest House Publishers, Inc., is the exclusive licensee of this trademark.

The Non-Prophet's Guide™ to the Book of Daniel
Copyright © 2023—Text © Todd Hampson, Artwork © Todd Hampson
Published by Harvest House Publishers
Eugene, Oregon 97408
www.harvesthousepublishers.com
ISBN 978-0-7369-8740-0 (pbk)
ISBN 978-0-7369-8741-7 (eBook)
Library of Congress Control Number: 2023934128

Printed in the United States of America

23 24 25 26 27 28 29 30 31 / VP / 10 9 8 7 6 5 4 3 2 1

Dedicated to Daniel, Maddie, (and our future grandchildren).
Tracey and I were studying the book of Daniel when we first discovered we were
to become parents. We decided to give you his namesake because of all that it
stands for. We made the right call and are so very proud of you and Maddie.

CONTENTS

SECTION 3: Yet-Future Prophecy

SECTION 4: Application

INTRODUCTION

More Relevant Now Than Ever

*We will never find any basis for charges against this man
Daniel unless it has something to do with the law of his God.*

DANIEL 6:5

The storm was intense. Lightning lit up the sky as the violent weather rattled the large passenger plane. The sound of the jet engines, combined with the wind and thunder, produced a fearful symphony. A couple sitting in the back of the plane wished they had seats closer to the front.

Not because it would take less time for them to disembark the plane, but it would negate the vulnerability they felt sitting in the very last row as the plane cut its way through the mammoth storm at more than 33,000 feet in the air.

Similar to being seated in the last car on a roller coaster, the two passengers felt the sudden drops a lot more than the lucky souls who sat in front of them. Furthermore, the back-row occupants observed the heads of a few hundred people jolting up and down in unison with each pocket of dead air or sudden gust of wind the plane encountered. This was not your average turbulence—the sort that provides mild tummy tickles joined by momentary fear and adrenaline. No, this was different. It was the kind of shaking they could feel in their hips as the plane suddenly yanked them down by the seatbelt.

The two weary back-row passengers put on a bold front for each other, but both were genuinely nervous behind their reassuring facial expressions. Neither had experienced this level of turbulence before. Neither had flown through such an intense thunderstorm while hurtling through the air at a few hundred miles an hour. Voices on the plane were minimal aside from the occasional gasps and a few young children crying. Fear was palpable. The couple felt the weight of the moment.

As they assessed the situation, they observed that behind them, just around the corner of the back wall, sat the three flight attendants. Each sat in a small flip-down seat with a seat belt across their lap. The three of them were quietly conversing, but not in fearful, hushed tones. Rather, they were laughing. Talking about everyday things. Chit-chatting about their lives and whatever else flight attendants talk to each other about.

The couple in the back row began to realize that the seasoned flight attendants had been through this before. Somehow the calm airline employees had confidence in both the pilot's ability and the integrity of the large plane. The fearlessness of the flight attendants was contagious, giving the young couple the sense that the pilot was trained for this—and that the plane was built for this. The entire crew of the airplane had already been trained and tested by similar storms. They were able to have confidence and joy in the middle of the storm.

What had seemed such an inconvenience to the couple suddenly became an unexpected comfort. The vulnerable and uneasy feeling of being in the back of the plane was replaced by a confident anchor of hope as they witnessed the demeanor of the calm flight attendants. As most of the other passengers continued to gasp and react to each new punch from the storm, the young couple weathered the rest of the flight with a sense of confidence and hope as they allowed the veteran courage of the flight attendants to impact their expectations.

This was the situation my son and his now-wife found themselves in during a trip with her family to Colorado a few years ago. On the way back to

Georgia, the plane encountered a serious storm that was so large they had no option but to fly straight through the heart of the atmosphere-hogging tempest. Perhaps you can relate. Maybe you feel like you are in a storm—with no way out but through the turbulent winds and terrifying lightning.

Unless you have been in a coma, living off the grid, or on an extended space mission for the past several years, you have witnessed firsthand how rapidly the world has become unstable on every significant level. The global effects resulting from COVID-19. The eroding of freedoms once held dear. Dictatorial governmental overreach. Lawlessness spanning from the streets to the highest levels of the government.

The downward spiral of upside-down delusional thinking seems to be descending more rapidly. Facts, logic, and common sense seem to be eroding as an increasing number of people are bowing to godless groupthink driven by deception and fear. Good is now seen as evil—and evil as good. Like no other time in history, since the flood of Noah's day or the Tower of Babel, have events had such a devastating global effect.

Now more than ever, as Christians we need to understand our times and to know how to live. For these reasons, I believe a careful study of the book of Daniel is greatly needed in our day. In it we can discover how to thrive during unstable times, and we can learn God's clear prophetic plans for every key plot point from Daniel's day all the way to the time of the end.

This raises a key question. Is the book of Daniel a book of practical godly living, or is it a book of prophecy? The answer is…yes! I've seen people focus on one to the detriment of the other. When it comes to the book of Daniel, it seems that teachers and authors tend to focus on either prophecy or the practical Christian living aspects of Daniel's record, but this shouldn't be the case. Both are represented in Daniel. The first six chapters are historical narrative (with much personal application to be gleaned), and the last six chapters are full of prophecy!

Let us not forget that God's prophetic Word is practical. Studying prophecy strengthens our faith in a God who keeps his promises. It also prepares us for the future. The prophecies of Daniel were given in the context of victorious godly living in the midst of a pagan culture and a horrible situation. We can't throw the baby out with the bathwater when it comes to teaching the whole counsel of God. We can't pick and choose what to teach and what to avoid when it comes to Scripture.

The book of Daniel is more relevant now than ever. As I alluded to above, the world and the West are becoming increasingly pagan, godless, and anti-Christian. America is on a fast-track downhill slide well into the delusional thinking described in Romans chapter 1. Based on the second half of Romans 1, America—as much as I love her—is already (in my opinion) under God's abandonment judgment. This is not God's active wrath as will happen during the future tribulation period, but it is a gentleman's judgment based on Romans chapter 1.

What I mean by that is this: God never forces his way or his will on people. As a country, we have systematically kicked God out of every aspect of culture and replaced him with cheap pagan counterfeits and embraced an ever-increasing depth of immorality at every turn. There is now no respect for the innocence of children, no respect for godly principles, and an increasing hostility toward every foundational truth of the Christian faith. As our nation systematically pushes God away, it also pushes away his protection, wisdom, blessing.

What we see today is exactly what the Bible tells us the end times would look like. In 2 Timothy 3:1-5, we read,

> Mark this: There will be terrible times in the last days. People will be lovers of themselves, lovers of money, boastful, proud, abusive, disobedient to their parents, ungrateful, unholy, without love, unforgiving, slanderous, without self-control, brutal, not lovers of the good, treacherous, rash, conceited, lovers of pleasure rather than lovers of God—having a form of godliness but denying its power. Have nothing to do with such people.

So, what is the Christian left to do in our day? Become pessimistic? Go live off the grid? Recoil into holy huddles and curse the darkness? Go on a rant judging the world for being the world? Cower in fear and do nothing? Embrace the immorality and incorporate it into a new, updated brand of faux Christianity? Seriously, these are some of the confusing and divergent options many believers have chosen for themselves in response to what is going on in the world around them. I believe there is a different way—a path that allows Christians to thrive and embrace the moment. We are not living during these times by accident. God. Is. Sovereign. That is the key message of the book of Daniel, and it is the most practical truth we can lean into right now in this moment of history.

Daniel lived at a time of rapid change (and judgment) after a prolonged period of grace and warning from God through his prophets. From a human perspective, Daniel's world was falling apart. The prophet's home country was decimated and he was forcibly taken to enemy territory to serve in a pagan, godless, violent, and immoral setting. This was not theoretical. It was Daniel's real-life situation. Yet God used him amid all the godlessness.

In fact, the harsh reality of Daniel's predicament provided the perfect opportunity for God to move the dial in a major way. The sweeping prophecies in the book of Daniel provide the biblical framework needed to understand the context of the New Testament, Jesus' teaching about the end times through his kingdom-focused parables and the Olivet Discourse, and the oft-avoided book of Revelation. This can't be overstated—Daniel contains the foundational framework for an accurate understanding of the end times.

DANIEL

The book of Daniel also provides some of the most practical lessons one can find on how to survive and thrive during a period of rapid change while living in a culture that is antagonistic to the truths of Scripture and the ways of God. Daniel and a few of his friends navigated the complex situation they found themselves in and avoided godless indoctrination and forced false worship. They knew where the line in the sand was and stood up for God regardless of the possible negative outcomes. By doing so, they witnessed God do miracles. They walked through flames unscathed with the Son of God, saw the mouths of hungry lions remain shut, and talked face to face with God's supernatural messengers.

I believe we have entered a period of history that will result in two things: (1) the rapture of the church, and (2) increased global instability, Christian persecution, and antisemitism. The book of Daniel will prepare you for both! The practical lessons will equip you to stand firm as a believer—to know which lines in the sand must not be crossed. And the prophecies of Daniel will reveal God's faithful hand at work through history, helping you understand the details and the importance of the end times—for which we are watching the stage being so clearly set!

If you want to discover your calling, understand the context behind this current period in history, and thrive like never before—regardless of what is going on around you—then turn the page and let us begin a gritty, practical, and timely study in the book of Daniel. We need to reclaim a practical understanding of the sovereignty of God. Even in the midst of encroaching darkness and evil, we can still rest in God's unfailing love, provision, comfort, and joy. So, take courage as you carefully study the lessons, practical theology, and prophecies of the book of Daniel. God is the sovereign pilot who navigates the storm, and you were built for such a time as this.

The Non-Prophet

He's a Renaissance man. The ultimate throwback. The Non-Prophet is a 501(c)(3) that seems to have been born in 501 BC. He prefers the clothing, speech, food, facial grooming (or lack thereof), and customs of an archetypical Old Testament prophet living in twenty-first-century America. He misunderstands Bible prophecy and gives well-meaning but poor advice. The Non-Prophet is also not very wise with money, so he's a Non-Prophet on two levels. He's the epitome of the idiom "a day late and a dollar short."

SECTION 1:

HIS-STORY

SECTION 1:
HIS-STORY

SECTION 2:
FULFILLED PROPHECY

SECTION 3:
YET-FUTURE PROPHECY

SECTION 4:
APPLICATION

As mentioned in the introduction, Daniel is half historical narrative and half prophecy. Within that basic framework, *The Non-Prophet's Guide™ to the Book of Daniel* has four sections. The first seven chapters—Section 1—are dedicated to Daniel's historical narrative. History really is *his* story! God is the sovereign Master and Commander, and his story plays out in all of history! Then, chapters 8–15—Sections 2 and 3—cover the mind-blowing prophecies Daniel recorded for us some 2,600 years ago. Fulfilled prophecies are covered in section 2 and yet-future prophecies are covered in section 3. Finally, practical application of the book of Daniel is addressed in chapters 16–18—section 4.

As you'll see, the historical narrative provides the necessary background to more fully understand and appreciate both the prophecies in the book of Daniel, as well as, the practical applications of everything we'll study together. Now back to your regularly scheduled book.

SO HALF OF DANIEL IS COMEDY?

HISTORICAL NARRATIVE, NP. NOT HYSTERICAL.

MASTER OF BIBLE TERMS.

OH, RIGHT. PFFFT. I WAS JUST JOKING. GET IT?

CHAPTER 1

Kingdom Context

The God of heaven will set up a kingdom that will never be destroyed, nor will it be left to another people. It will crush all those kingdoms and bring them to an end, but it will itself endure forever.

DANIEL 2:44

When I was growing up in the 1970s and 1980s, there were primarily three types of glue: Elmer's Glue, Rubber Cement, and Krazy Glue. Elmer's Glue is packaged in a white bottle with a signature orange pointed cap. Every elementary school student had a bottle that could be found in their backpack or desk. This glue was intended to be used to make a collage, build a structure out of popsicle sticks, adhere cotton ball clouds to the inside of a diorama, or any number of other educational crafts one may imagine.

We children of the '80s also invented other non-intended uses for this magical substance. My favorite was the hand pocket. After applying a few thin layers of Elmer's Glue to our palms and allowing it adequate time to dry—we would then gently and meticulously peel the glue pocket open, from the top of the palm downward. If one was patient enough, they would end up with a nice pocket made of glue that was suitable for accommodating two full-sized square rubber erasers, a folded-up piece of paper, roughly 83 cents worth of change, or even a small action figure. Hardly practical, but immensely entertaining—the Elmer's Glue palm pocket is a nostalgic part of my elementary school career. Fast-forward to today, and there is a vast array of glues available in craft and hardware stores, made for every conceivable purpose including adhesives that bind metal, cement, rubber, plastic, cloth, and more.

The Bible has different types of glue as well. It is one grand narrative from Genesis to Revelation, yet it is held together through various strings of connective literary and theological fiber. I have highlighted this fact in a few of my other books by detailing things such as the scarlet thread of redemption that points to Jesus spanning from Genesis 3:15 all the way to the last chapter of Revelation.

I also cite what I refer to as the Central Nervous System (CNS) of the Bible—prophecy! Both the scarlet thread (details pointing to the Messiah and his redemptive work) and the CNS of the Bible (which connects each key story, person, event, and line of theology) are present in the book of Daniel.

Yet there is another type of supernatural adhesive that runs through Scripture and plays a key role in the book of Daniel. Daniel helps highlight that on a certain level, the Bible is a book of kingdoms.

Daniel's Glue

In Daniel, the eternal kingdom of God is juxtaposed against the counterfeit kingdom of Satan—the "god of this age," the "ruler of this world," and the "prince of the power of the air." Satan's rule has played out in real history through the Gentile kingdoms of the world. These temporal kingdoms stand in stark contrast to the future millennial kingdom, when Christ will literally rule the world from Jerusalem for 1,000 years, as an overture to God's everlasting kingdom. This kingdom theme fits the contextual narrative of Daniel, who was taken captive from the kingdom of Judah and taken to the heart of the superpower of the day—the Babylonian Empire. Ultimately, this kingdom context is a theme that points to the absolute sovereignty of God over the affairs of mankind.

Here in the book of Daniel, the glue of the kingdom narrative appears on center stage. Daniel was an exilic prophet—taken captive from Judah to Babylon in 605 BC. (In the next chapter, we will see a more complete background to the book of Daniel.) Viewing Daniel through this lens helps frame the narrative and prophecies found within its pages.

Here are select verses from Daniel that highlight this kingdom theme:

> 2:44—"In the time of those kings, the God of heaven will set up a kingdom that will never be destroyed, nor will it be left to another people. It will crush all those kingdoms and bring them to an end, but it will itself endure forever."

4:3—"His kingdom is an eternal kingdom; his dominion endures from generation to generation."

4:25—"Seven times will pass by for you until you acknowledge that the Most High is sovereign over all kingdoms on earth and gives them to anyone he wishes."

6:26—"He is the living God and he endures forever; his kingdom will not be destroyed, his dominion will never end."

7:18—"The holy people of the Most High will receive the kingdom and will possess it forever—yes, for ever and ever."

7:27—"The sovereignty, power and greatness of all the kingdoms under heaven will be handed over to the holy people of the Most High. His kingdom will be an everlasting kingdom, and all rulers will worship and obey him."

This kingdom theme is picked up in the New Testament as well. In Matthew 3, John the Baptist—aware of his role of preparing the way for the Messiah—called on people to repent, proclaiming that "the kingdom of heaven has come near" (Matthew 3:2). After Jesus was baptized by John, he went immediately to the desert to be tempted by Satan. In Matthew 4:8-9, Satan offered Jesus "all the kingdoms of the world." In Luke 11:20 and 17:21, Jesus told the rebellious religious leaders that the kingdom of God had come upon them and that it was "in their midst." Jesus is God and brought the kingdom—the sovereign rule of God—wherever he went. Everywhere Jesus walked, the kingdom of God went with him.

PHARISEES & SADDUCEES

The religious leaders of the day—the Pharisees and Sadducees—were expecting a physical kingdom that would overthrow Rome. They had read and studied the many Old Testament prophecies of a future descendant of David ruling from Jerusalem in a literal, physical kingdom. Those prophecies will be fulfilled in the future millennial kingdom (Revelation 20:1-7), but in Luke 17, Jesus was essentially telling them, *you are looking for an earthly kingdom but the King of kings is standing here in front of you and you don't even realize it.* God in flesh stood before the top religious leaders of the day and they had no clue.

Even when Jesus spoke to the crowds and taught his disciples, he had a kingdom focus. In fact, every one of Jesus' parables recorded in Scripture were in some way related to the future, literal, physical kingdom.

This kingdom theme is evident throughout Jesus' ministry, all the way to the cross. Each of the four gospel accounts (Matthew 27:37, Mark 15:26, Luke 23:38, and John 19:19) record the details about the sign placed upon the cross of Jesus, which referred to him as "The King of the Jews."

THE FUTURE KINGDOM AGE

HERE ARE A FEW VERSES THAT PROVIDE KEY DETAILS ABOUT THE JEWISH PEOPLE RETURNING TO THE LAND AND A LITERAL FUTURE KINGDOM.

Deuteronomy 30:1-10
Psalm 2:6-8
Psalm 89:3-4, 19-37
Isaiah 2:1-4
Isaiah 9:6-7
Isaiah 11:1-9
Isaiah 26:1-4
Isaiah 35:1-10
Isaiah 49:19-26
Isaiah 60:1-22
Isaiah 65:20-25
Jeremiah 23:5-6
Jeremiah 31:31-34
Jeremiah 32:38-39
Jeremiah 33:6-9
Jeremiah 33:15-18
Ezekiel 36:25-28
Ezekiel 37:15-23
Ezekiel 43:1-7
Ezekiel 47:1-12
Ezekiel 48:8-20
Ezekiel 48:30-35
Joel 3:17-21
Amos 9:11-15
Micah 4:1-8
Zechariah 8:1-17
Zechariah 14:6-21
Matthew 19:28
Luke 22:28-30
2 Timothy 2:12
Revelation 20:1-10

So, is the kingdom of God in Jesus? in Heaven? in each believer? or a future kingdom on earth? The answer is…yes! All of these are true. God is sovereign over all, so his kingdom extends everywhere. Within the bounds of God's sovereign rule, he has mysteriously allowed the fall of man and the placement of the world under Satan's temporary rule. The book of Revelation details Jesus' reclaiming of the world. After the tribulation period, Christ will return, and he will set up the millennial kingdom—a literal future Kingdom.

Here in the book of Daniel, we become witnesses to history told in advance, seeing the world's mighty superpowers pridefully march toward their predicted outcomes and under the ultimate sovereign rule of God. Theologians have stated that the devil is God's devil—he is being used as a tool to bring about a result. So, even a fallen world under the dominion of Satan is playing into God's overall sovereign plan—when he will take back the title deed to the world and set up a literal kingdom on earth.

We can say, in one sense, the book of Daniel is a story about kingdoms. It compares earthly kingdoms with the kingdom of God. We will look at this in greater detail in the chapters that follow—particularly as we study Daniel chapters 2 and 7. When describing the book of Daniel, one writer puts it this way: "Daniel is preeminently the book of the sovereignty of God over the kingdoms of men."[1]

The Contextual Crux of the Issue

So, the underlying principle at work through the kingdom context is the sovereignty of God. As you consider the context of the book of Daniel, it is important to remember that it was written at a point in Israel's history when all seemed lost. Nothing was going right. The darkest of times had fallen on the nation. The people were hopeless. God seemed absent and his promises seemed to have failed.

But even when all seems lost, God is just as sovereign as ever. God's plans are not hindered by free will, rebellious leaders, evil plans, and seemingly unexpected setbacks. The ultimate drive behind the book of Daniel was God reminding his people that he alone is the sovereign ruler of the universe.

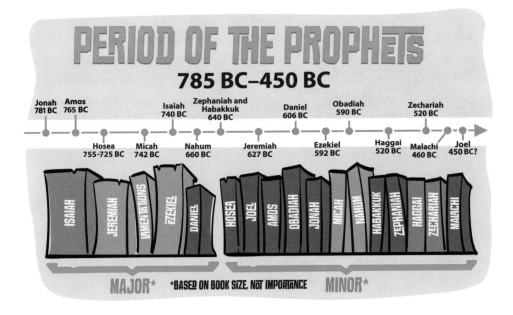

PERIOD OF THE PROPHETS
785 BC–450 BC

Jonah 781 BC
Amos 765 BC
Isaiah 740 BC
Zephaniah and Habakkuk 640 BC
Daniel 606 BC
Obadiah 590 BC
Zechariah 520 BC

Hosea 755-725 BC
Micah 742 BC
Nahum 660 BC
Jeremiah 627 BC
Ezekiel 592 BC
Haggai 520 BC
Malachi 460 BC
Joel 450 BC?

ISAIAH · JEREMIAH · LAMENTATIONS · EZEKIEL · DANIEL · HOSEA · JOEL · AMOS · OBADIAH · JONAH · MICAH · NAHUM · HABAKKUK · ZEPHANIAH · HAGGAI · ZECHARIAH · MALACHI

MAJOR*   *BASED ON BOOK SIZE, NOT IMPORTANCE   MINOR*

There is an inherent tension—a paradox, if you will—in Scripture between man's responsibility (free will) and God's sovereignty. God is ultimately in charge of every single detail of history. If there were a single rogue atom or irregular length of Planck time (the shortest mathematical duration known to man), God would not be sovereign. By definition, God is either completely and fully sovereign, or not sovereign at all. If anything seen or unseen is outside of God's ultimate control, he is not the sovereign ruler of the cosmos.

Yet, at the same time, moral beings have a free will. Both humans and angels (at least prior to the initial rebellion in heaven) can choose to follow God or to reject him. We are responsible for our thoughts, actions, and choices. Volumes have been written about this paradox, but the bottom line is that every key theological concept has an inherent paradox. For example, God is three distinct persons (Father, Son, and Holy Spirit), yet he is one God. As believers, we live our Christian lives, yet Christ lives them through us (Galatians 2:20). We choose to respond to God, yet at the same time, he chooses us. We freely choose our actions, yet every single day of our lives has been prerecorded (Psalm 139:16).

Much of this has to do with two things. First, God is outside of time and already knows everything in our future. Second, God is God and we are not. The moment we try to "figure out" God is the moment we lose sight of his otherworldliness— his divine nature. Simply put, we cannot contain the Creator of the Universe in the space between our ears. He is so far beyond us that we can't fathom his ways. Yet he loves us so much that he communicates with us, died for us, and is intimately involved in every detail of our lives. What a wonderful God!

The harsh reality of Daniel's situation provided the perfect platform for God to share a bigger picture of his plans than anyone had ever previously known. You will see this as we move through the book. It's evident in every chapter of Daniel's record, and most notably in Daniel chapters 2, 7, and 9. During a time when Israel had hit absolute rock bottom, God used Daniel to remind them (and us, as we study the text) that God is still in control and his plans are still firmly in place.

CHAPTER 2

The Background

In the third year of the reign of Jehoiakim king of Judah, Nebuchadnezzar king of Babylon came to Jerusalem and besieged it. And the Lord delivered Jehoiakim king of Judah into his hand, along with some of the articles from the temple of God. These he carried off to the temple of his god in Babylonia and put in the treasure house of his god.

DANIEL 1:1-2

Focus: Record of Babylonian captivity and prophecies about Israel's entire future

Author: Daniel

Book Date: 537 BC

Narrative Timeframe Covered: 605 BC–537 BC

Prophetic Timeframe Covered: 605 BC to the yet-future millennial kingdom

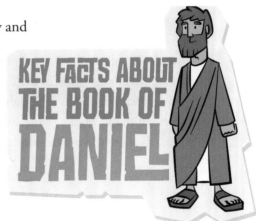

KEY FACTS ABOUT THE BOOK OF DANIEL

Place of Ministry: To the exiles in Babylon

Practical Lessons:

- God honors a life of faithfulness
- Through obedience we can thrive even in a hostile environment
- Standing on God's truth is always the best choice
- God's prophetic Word always proves true

Main Overarching Theme: The sovereignty of God

The Bible is one mega-story. One grand narrative. If you have read any of my other books, you'll recall that I mention this quite often. Now, when I say the Bible is a story, I do not mean it is fabricated. The Bible is the most verified ancient document in existence. History and archeology continuously confirm details that are recorded in Scripture. The book of Daniel, in particular, is so accurate in its details, dates, and prophecies that critics of the Bible used to say it had to have been written after the fulfilled prophecies had occurred, but we will address this in more detail in chapter 9!

In its most basic form, a good story has three components: set-up, conflict, and resolution. Without the set-up, the conflict loses its punch. Without the set-up, the resolution has so much less meaning. You might say the Bible is a basic story of creation, fall, redemption. Set-up, conflict, resolution. But within that grand scope are many subplots, story arcs, aspects of rising tension, and rabbit trails that always make their way back into the grand narrative of creation, fall, and redemption.

The book of Daniel falls within one of those trails. It is found in the section of the Old Testament known as the "Major Prophets." The major and minor prophets both fall chronologically within the historical section of the Old Testament. The designation of major and minor relate merely to a book's size, not its importance. Isaiah, Jeremiah, Lamentations, Ezekiel, and Daniel are the largest of the 17 books of the prophets canonized in the Old Testament; therefore, they are the major prophets.

Key to any story is an understanding of the set-up. The background is fundamental to following and appreciating both the narrative and the practical application of Scripture. Now that we've discussed context, we can address the details of the background. This chapter is foundational to the rest of this book. It contains key information that will inform the remaining chapters. In short, it provides the critical context you will need to get the most out of your study of the book of Daniel—a key book of prophecy and practical application.

Of the 16 prophets who have books named after them in the Old Testament, Daniel is one of only three whose ministry took place during the exile. Most of the prophets lived before the exile (see chart below) and warned of God's coming judgment if the nations of Israel and Judah did not repent.

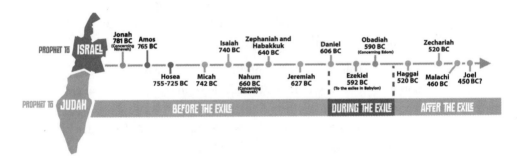

In many ways, the book of Daniel is the second part to the book of Jeremiah. Jeremiah—who was in his older years when Daniel was a teenager—had the rare (and heartbreaking) privilege of warning the people of Judah of impending judgment and living to witness it himself. He warned specifically that Babylon would attack and conquer the nation of Judah. In Jeremiah 25:9, we read God's words through the prophet declaring,

> "I will summon all the peoples of the north and my servant Nebuchadnezzar king of Babylon," declares the Lord, "and I will bring them against this land and its inhabitants and against all the surrounding nations. I will completely destroy them and make them an object of horror and scorn, and an everlasting ruin."

This prophecy was fulfilled and Jeremiah survived the judgment. The prophet recorded his eyewitness account in the book of Lamentations. He is known as the "weeping prophet" because of his raw and unfiltered description of what he witnessed and how it impacted him. To understand what led up to Daniel's captivity in Judah, you may want to read Jeremiah 39–40 and the book of Lamentations.

The Bible is a supernatural book of theology, but it is also an accurate record of history. In Jeremiah 52, we're given the specific dates of the Babylonian attack and the duration of the siege. We also learn the dates of, and the numbers of people taken in, each of the three expulsions to Babylon.

> 52:4-5—"In the ninth year of Zedekiah's reign, on the tenth day of the tenth month, Nebuchadnezzar king of Babylon marched against Jerusalem with his whole army. They encamped outside the city and built siege works all around it. The city was kept under siege until the eleventh year of King Zedekiah."

> 52:28-30—"This is the number of the people Nebuchadnezzar carried into exile: in the seventh year, 3,023 Jews; in Nebuchadnezzar's eighteenth year, 832 people from Jerusalem; in his twenty-third year, 745 Jews taken into exile by Nebuzaradan the commander of the imperial guard. There were 4,600 people in all."

Daniel was a young man (probably a teenager) when he was taken to Babylon. He was from a noble family of Judah (Daniel 1:3-4) and was exiled in 605 BC, during the first of the three deportations cited above (605, 597, and 586 BC). Upon arrival, he was renamed Belteshazzar (named after one of the Babylonian gods—Bel) as part of the indoctrination process that the Babylonian leadership used to integrate conquered peoples into the Babylonian way of life. We learn that three of Daniel's friends—Hananiah, Mishael, and Azariah—also had their names changed to Shadrach, Meshach, and Abednego. It was forced assimilation. But as we'll see in the next two chapters of this book, Daniel and his three friends refused to conform to the ungodly practices of the Babylonians.

DANIEL NAME MEANING "GOD IS MY JUDGE"

BELTESHAZZAR NAME MEANING "BEL PROTECTS HIS LIFE"

Daniel lived in Babylon for the entire 70-year captivity (Daniel 1:21; 9:2), which was—again—prophesied by Jeremiah (Jeremiah 25:11-12; 29:10). The concise details of God's warnings to Judah prior to the captivity, the devastation caused by the Babylonians, the state of the land and the exiles all the way through the captivity, and the return of the exiles to the land are recorded for us in 2 Chronicles 36:15-23. We have the privilege of hindsight—seeing the entire captivity and return. Daniel did not. He experienced it as each day unfolded, one at a time, for 70 years. The book of Daniel is the record of his experiences and how God used him as a prophet during the darkest of times.

Details of Daniel's Exile:

- Taken captive in 605 BC
- Served in public roles until 538 BC (Daniel 1:21)
- Served as a prophet until at least 536 BC (Daniel 10:1)
- 70-year ministry (entire Babylonian captivity)
- Most likely lived well into his 80s

The Uniqueness of the Book

The book of Daniel is quite unique among other books of the Bible in that it is a book of both history and prophecy. As I alluded to in the introduction of this book, a very basic outline of the book of Daniel have it split into two major sections or literary categories. The first six chapters are historical narrative. The last six chapters are in the prophecy genre. One caveat to keep in mind is that, within that basic framework, we do find prophecy in the narrative section and narrative in the prophetic section. The basic outline only shows the primary genre or focus of those two sections.

The book of Daniel can be called the "Revelation" of the Old Testament. It sets the tone for the language and much of the symbolism used later in the Bible, in the book of Revelation. Daniel provides the overarching structure that all other scriptural end-times passages fit into. Most readers are familiar with the narrative sections of Daniel: the lions' den, the fiery furnace, the handwriting on the wall, etc. Those are indeed incredible historical sections with relevant application for us today, providing insight and encouragement that shows believers how to remain faithful to the Lord in godless foreign territory.

Surrounding those wonderful narrative sections from the book of Daniel we also find a lot of prophecy. Of the 12 chapters in Daniel, eight of them contain prophecy—a whopping two-thirds of the book. Written around 537 BC, the book of Daniel accurately details the four successive kingdoms starting from the Babylonian Empire through to the Roman Empire, and a clear description of Europe during "the time of the end." Daniel chapter 9 (particularly the last four verses) details Israel's entire prophetic history from Daniel's time through to the future tribulation period, and ultimately into the millennial kingdom!

Here is a more detailed and specific breakdown outlined below.

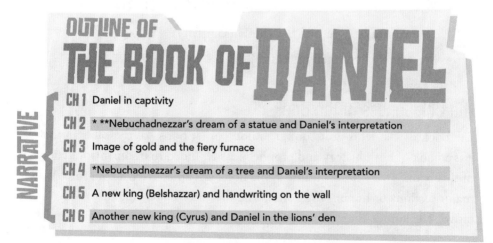

OUTLINE OF
THE BOOK OF DANIEL

NARRATIVE

CH 1 Daniel in captivity

CH 2 * **Nebuchadnezzar's dream of a statue and Daniel's interpretation

CH 3 Image of gold and the fiery furnace

CH 4 *Nebuchadnezzar's dream of a tree and Daniel's interpretation

CH 5 A new king (Belshazzar) and handwriting on the wall

CH 6 Another new king (Cyrus) and Daniel in the lions' den

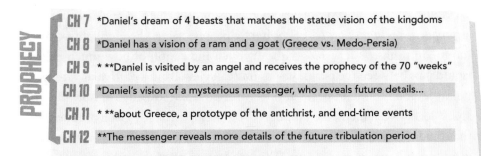

*contains future prophecy from Daniel's perspective
** contains end-times-specific prophecy from our perspective

The first six chapters (narrative section) tell the historical account of Daniel living as a captive in Babylon from his teenage years into his old age. These chapters span a timeline of 70 years and three different rulers of Babylon. Within the first section, Daniel interprets two of Nebuchadnezzar's dreams and provides detailed prophecies. The last six chapters of Daniel (prophetic section) consists of various prophecies given directly to Daniel through dreams, visions, and communication with angels.

Here's another fascinating fact related to the organization of the book of Daniel—specific sections were not written chronologically. Instead, they are organized into distinct sections that relate to Israel and to the Gentile (non-Jewish) nations. Interestingly, chapter 1 is written in Hebrew, chapters 2–7 are written in Aramaic—the Gentile language of the day—and chapters 8–12 switch back to Hebrew. The language used in each section is directly related to the people group impacted by the prophecies contained in those chapters. Since Daniel was captive in a Gentile region, it is likely he wanted to make sure those who lived there could understand his writings. And Jewish people in Daniel's day could read both the Aramaic and Hebrew languages.

QUICK FACT: DID YOU KNOW...

that Daniel understood their captivity would be 70 years (9:2) by studying Jeremiah 25:11-12?

When it comes to Bible prophecy, there is a concept that theologians refer to as *prophetic mountain peaks*. Very often, a prophecy hits the highlights—the mountain peaks, as it were—without much indication of how much time would pass between the peaks. Just as one can view, from a particular vantage point, several mountain peaks at once with no real knowledge of how much space lies between them, the prophets of old were frequently given prophecies that predicted key events but offered no real indication of how much time would span between said events. This concept of prophetic mountain peaks comes into play with certain prophecies found in Daniel. In several places, you'll read a prophecy about world events, then in the next phrase or sentence, Daniel abruptly switches his focus to future end-times events. Daniel also provides many key details about the evil end-times ruler we often refer to as the antichrist (though that term is only used four times in Scripture: 1 John 2:18, 22; 4:3; 2 John 7).

THE MOUNTAIN PEAKS OF BIBLE PROPHECY

FRONT VIEW   SIDE VIEW

Foundational Eschatology

As mentioned above, the book of Daniel is—in many ways—the "Revelation" of the Old Testament. It forms the basic framework for other key eschatological (related to the study of last things) sections of Scripture that provide more details about the time of the end.

In college, my drawing instructors always taught that in order to produce a good piece of artwork, we students needed to "bring up" the whole drawing together. Unless it is an intentional stylistic choice, a well-trained artist won't just pick one spot on the paper and immediately begin drawing fine details before moving to other areas to render.

Artists are taught to build the framework of a composition first, beginning with broad strokes and loose gestures, while using their entire arm to rough out a full sketch. An artist must think about composition, positive and negative space, proportions, line of action, and other considerations as they work and rework their art, loosely at first.

Once an artist has adequately addressed those foundational considerations, they can confidently commit to a clean sketch using bold, defining strokes that clearly frame the composition. Finally, once that key framework is committed to paper, the artist can continue bringing up the whole piece by adding shading and highlights, and finally, by adding fine details using the smaller, more coordinated muscles of the hand and fingers.

Studying prophecy is much the same. Students of Bible prophecy need to begin by familiarizing themselves with the entire Bible. Old Testament books like Daniel and Ezekiel lay down large foundational strokes of key information. Then other Old Testament books, like the books of the minor prophets and passages in Psalms, add more framework and proportion with other key information.

Then the Gospels and letters of the New Testament shine a bright light on and provide definition to many mysterious details that were veiled in the Old Testament. What was concealed in the Old Testament, the New Testament now reveals. Mysteries like the rapture and the gap between the first and second comings of Christ, for example, have only been made clearly known to us in the New Testament writings. Finally, the book of Revelation rounds out our prophetic understanding, effectively tying together every key theme in the Bible in stark detail.

The Critical Context of the Covenants

If you know anyone who works in real estate, you have probably heard the three most important factors in relation to the value of a property—location, location, location! Far above any other factor, when determining the price of a home, is location. Likewise, there is a similar rule in Bible interpretation (also known as hermeneutics). Far above anything else, when interpreting Scripture, is context, context, context.

When you are studying a passage of Scripture, first, it is important to understand the context of the book (in this case, the book of Daniel). Second, it is imperative to comprehend the context of the section of the Bible where the book is found (in this case, the books of the prophets in the Old Testament). Third, it is critical to understand the context of the entire work (in this case, the completed canon of the entire Bible).

Earlier, I provided the general context for the book of Daniel and the time of the prophets, but in order to fully understand the narrative and prophecies of Daniel, I thought it would be valuable to provide a broader overview of the full context and how it fits into the overall story of Scripture. In the grand narrative of the Bible, the book of Daniel is better understood in the context of Old Testament Jewish history. More specifically, understood in light of God's covenants between himself and the Jewish people. In very broadbrush terms, Daniel is the record of the results of Israel's disobedience as well as her promised future.

After creation, the fall, the flood, and the Tower of Babel, God called Abram (later renamed Abraham) out of a polytheistic culture and established an unconditional covenant with him (Genesis 12:1-3), which promised descendants, a land, and a future worldwide blessing. This covenant was confirmed with Abraham's son Isaac and his grandson Jacob.

Jacob's 12 sons became the heads of 12 tribes who grew into a large nation in Egypt, where a new ruler arose and enslaved them. This led to the events surrounding Moses, including the exodus, the giving of the law (the Mosaic covenant, Exodus 19–24), and the eventual taking of the promised land.

Unlike the Abrahamic covenant, the Mosaic covenant was conditional. Its purpose was to inform the Jewish people how they were to live in the promised land. It was given for a specific time period and promised blessings for obedience and punishment for disobedience. An understanding of Deuteronomy 28 is key here. In that single chapter (as well as other sections of Numbers and Deuteronomy), God lays out the specific blessings for obedience as well as the specific curses for disobedience.

MOSAIC COVENANT = CONDITIONAL
DEUTERONOMY 28

Following Israel's conquest of Canaan and after the death of Joshua, things began to fall apart. The people of Israel failed to obey all that God had commanded and fell into a time when "every man did what was right in his own eyes" (Judges 21:25 RSV). They completely disregarded the Mosaic law and the punishments foretold in Deuteronomy 28. This was the period of the judges—a lawless and chaotic period during which God had to continually rescue his people from the results of their own rebellion.

Then the people began to desire to have a king—like the nations around them—instead of letting God guide them through faithful obedience to the Mosaic law. God eventually gave them what they wanted. Through the last judge, Samuel (who was also a prophet), God installed Israel's first king—Saul. King Saul's failures and David's obedience to God resulted in David becoming Israel's most famous king.

In 2 Samuel 7, God initiated the Davidic covenant—another permanent and unconditional covenant. God promised that a future descendant of David would rule an everlasting kingdom. So, the conditional and temporary Mosaic covenant (as clearly laid out in Deuteronomy 28) was now sandwiched in between two unconditional and permanent covenants. The Abrahamic covenant, God's promise of a land, a people, and a world-wide blessing. And, the Davidic covenant, whereby a distant descendant of David would rule forever.

DAVIDIC COVENANT = UNCONDITIONAL
2 SAMUEL 7

The Lord declares to you that the Lord himself will establish a house for you: When your days are over and you rest with your ancestors, I will raise up your offspring to succeed you, your own flesh and blood, and I will establish his kingdom. He is the one who will build a house for my Name, and I will establish the throne of his kingdom forever. I will be his father, and he will be my son. When he does wrong, I will punish him with a rod wielded by men, with floggings inflicted by human hands. But my love will never be taken away from him, as I took it away from Saul, whom I removed from before you. Your house and your kingdom will endure forever before me; your throne will be established forever (2 Samuel 7:11-16).

King David thrived until the scandal with Bathsheba. Afterward, his life was a constant roller coaster of various struggles. David's son Solomon also started off strongly, but fell into idolatry after marrying foreign wives who led him astray. In other words, he was inviting the curses of Deuteronomy 28. Out of God's commitment to David, the results of the two kings' disobedience would be delayed until after Solomon died. And sure enough, Solomon's son ruled harshly and this resulted in a divided kingdom, with Israel in the north and Judah in the south. First and 2 Kings chronicle the continued disobedience of the two kingdoms. The northern kingdom had all evil rulers, while the southern kingdom had all evil rulers except (arguably) two or three good ones. Again, both kingdoms continued to violate Deuteronomy 28 and were therefore inviting the curses prophetically listed therein.

It is during this very period that God raised up prophets to call both nations back to God. The nations refused, and as a result, Israel was defeated by the Assyrians in 722 BC. The southern kingdom of Judah held on a little longer, but they were defeated by the Babylonians in

THE SPLIT KINGDOM

ISRAEL — DEFEATED BY THE ASSYRIANS 722 BC

JUDAH — DEFEATED BY THE BABYLONIANS 586 BC

586 BC. This history of unconditional and conditional covenants is the context in which Daniel was taken into captivity as a teenager. As I detailed above, he was one of three exilic prophets, meaning his ministry took place while the Jewish people were in exile.

There is one more covenant that was prophesied in the Old Testament—the new covenant. In Luke 22:20, during the first communion, Jesus identified it: "In the same way, after the supper he took the cup, saying, 'This cup is the new covenant in my blood, which is poured out for you.'" Many people read those words and don't realize Jesus was pointing back to another unconditional covenant God gave in Jeremiah 31:31-34 (see also Ezekiel 36:24-28; 37:14; Joel 2:28-29). We read this in Jeremiah 31:31-33:

> "The days are coming," declares the LORD, "when I will make a new covenant with the people of Israel and with the people of Judah. It will not be like the covenant I made with their ancestors when I took them by the hand to lead them out of Egypt, because they broke my covenant, though I was a husband to them," declares the LORD. "This is the covenant I will make with the people of Israel after that time," declares the LORD. "I will put my law in their minds and write it on their hearts. I will be their God, and they will be my people."

Recall Jesus' words early in his ministry, that he "was sent only to the lost sheep of Israel" (Matthew 15:24). Also recall that when Jesus first sent out the 12 disciples, he commanded them not to go to the Gentiles, but rather, "to the lost sheep of Israel" (Matthew 10:6). That is because the new covenant—the one that you and I are part of—is first and foremost an unconditional covenant specifically "with the people of Israel and with the people of Judah" (Jeremiah 31:31). God's main focus is always his original covenant people. Those of us in the church age, who are not Jewish, are grafted in. We are blessed by all three unconditional covenants, and even by the conditional Mosaic covenant. Israel's disobedience to the Mosaic covenant opened a way for non-Jewish people to be grafted in (Romans 11:17-20).

So, all four covenants set the stage for the book of Daniel. Understanding these covenants will help you understand the reason for Daniel's captivity, as well as the purposes of the prophecies that are foretold in the book of Daniel (particularly chapters 2, 7, and 9). Even though God's people were experiencing defeat and exile, God still promised that the Jewish people would have a people, a land, and a worldwide blessing. God also promised that a literal descendant of David would one day literally rule from Jerusalem in the promised land.

And God's promise that a day was coming when a new covenant would replace the old (Mosaic) covenant still held true. Furthermore, the conditional provisions of the Mosaic covenant proved to be prophetic. When the people of Israel and their leaders were obedient, they experienced God's blessing. When they were disobedient, they experienced the curses exactly as detailed in Deuteronomy 28. Daniel found himself in the worst of the storm—the result of the disobedience of his nation and his leaders.

Necessary Foundations

I know what I just shared is quite a lot of information, but I promise it will help provide the background and context for both the narrative and prophetic sections of the book of Daniel. So, as we dive into the next chapter, put yourself in Daniel's sandals. Imagine what it would have been like to witness the downfall of your nation by foreign powers, then to be taken from your home into captivity in a foreign, pagan land with no idea of what the future held—and all of this as a teenager! In the opening chapter of Daniel, we quickly learn the source of Daniel's strength, and how he was able to navigate the turbulent waters and live a godly life while going against the current.

CHAPTER 3

The Hero's Journey

Praise be to the name of God for ever and ever; wisdom and power are his. He changes times and seasons; he deposes kings and raises up others. He gives wisdom to the wise and knowledge to the discerning.

DANIEL 2:20-21

We are here.

DANIEL
1 2 3 4 5 6 7 8 9 10 11 12
HISTORICAL NARRATIVE   PREDICTIVE PROPHECY

Since we're using a story theme for Section 1 (His-Story) of this book, I thought it fitting to introduce (or reintroduce) you to the Hero's Journey for the opening of this chapter. The most famous explanation of the Hero's Journey was captured in a book by the American writer and literature professor Joseph Campbell in 1949. The book is called *The Hero with a Thousand Faces*. In it, Campbell shared his research of ancient stories and formalized the common elements that resonate with the human spirit and make for a good story. He demonstrated how a common general structure, revolving around a protagonist (the hero), seemed to be a universal human storytelling pattern. This oft-repeated story cycle is referred to as the monomyth, or (after Campbell's book was circulated) the hero's journey.

The concept of the hero's journey has since influenced storytellers of all professions—particularly novelists, filmmakers, and screenwriters.

The hero's journey has since been simplified, modified, and slightly reworked by other storytellers, but they all use the same basic chronological plot points that move the story forward and take the protagonist from ordinary to extraordinary.

The hero begins as an everyday person, is called (or taken) to adventure, leaves what is familiar, goes through various trials, faces his worst fear, and overcomes it. This journey results in new strengths and abilities that the hero brings back to his world to impact it in a new way. If you'll recall my story intro in the previous chapter, you'll notice that this follows the basic story pillars of setup, conflict, and resolution.

God is a storyteller, and we as humans are made in the image of God. That is why a good story resonates with us. Dogs and cats, for instance, do not contemplate story concepts or the hero's journey, but as humans, it is innately part of our nature. As previously mentioned, the Bible is one grand narrative—a monolithic story straight from the heart of the Storyteller of all storytellers.

The life of Daniel and the book he recorded for us follows the general pattern of the hero's journey. In the opening chapter of Daniel we jump onto a moving train. He has already left his normal and familiar life, having been taken captive to Babylon. If the book of Daniel were a feature film, the audience would be immediately dropped into an opening scene that begs explanation. It's clear that Daniel and his friends are uncomfortable and unfamiliar with their surroundings.

The opening verses of Daniel chapter 1 fill in the gaps and catch us up to speed. In five short verses, readers learn the details about the devastation of

Daniel's homeland and the massive transitions that have taken place. In Daniel 1:1-5, we read the following:

> In the third year of the reign of Jehoiakim king of Judah, Nebuchadnezzar king of Babylon came to Jerusalem and besieged it. And the Lord delivered Jehoiakim king of Judah into his hand, along with some of the articles from the temple of God. These he carried off to the temple of his god in Babylonia and put in the treasure house of his god. Then the king ordered Ashpenaz, chief of his court officials, to bring into the king's service some of the Israelites from the royal family and the nobility—young men without any physical defect, handsome, showing aptitude for every kind of learning, well informed, quick to understand, and qualified to serve in the king's palace. He was to teach them the language and literature of the Babylonians. The king assigned them a daily amount of food and wine from the king's table. They were to be trained for three years, and after that they were to enter the king's service.

Daniel's Twofold Training

Those opening verses inform us that Daniel was a high-caliber individual, whom the Babylonians tried to forcibly assimilate into their ways and their culture. They wanted to break him, and then retrain him. But, within that very situation, God's training was present as well. Daniel was a righteous young man. He was committed to God and the Mosaic law. He had read and studied Deuteronomy 28. He knew the consequences of disobedience. He had just witnessed them in action, when God allowed Judah—and beloved Jerusalem—to be ransacked and disrespected. Daniel also knew the upside of Deuteronomy 28—the blessings promised for obedience. Now in a foreign land, God's training ground was poised to move Daniel's faith from theoretical to actual. From ideas to actions.

Daniel and his three friends, Hananiah, Mishael, and Azariah (more commonly referred to by their Babylonian names—Shadrach, Meshach, and Abednego), seemed to be a band of brothers, so to speak. Right out of the gate, they chose to take a stand together, against the royal program, and asked not to be given the royal food and wine. Keep in mind that most scholars (based on ancient training practices and the time cues given in the book of Daniel) posit that Daniel and his friends were between 14 and 17 years of age. Yet they confidently stood up for their faith and their God. And Daniel led the way.

Apparently, the food and wine offered to Daniel and his friends had either been offered to the Babylonian gods as sacrifices before idols, or it did not meet the requirements of the Mosaic law—or perhaps both. Whatever the case, it was clear to Daniel that he would be disobeying God's clear instruction and going against his own conscience if he ate and drank from the king's table. Daniel addressed the matter directly with the official who was placed over the captives, and the Lord blessed Daniel and his friends in the process by causing the official to give them some leeway. Daniel bargained with him, asking for ten days of only being provided vegetables and water, and then to see how they fared at the end of this trial period. God worked miraculously behind the scenes, and at the end of the ten-day period, Daniel and his

friends were healthier than the rest of the young men drafted into the king's service, who were eating and drinking the royal food and wine. The phrase used for "healthier and better nourished" in verse 15 communicates a sense of being fairer and fatter.

This should be a reminder to us, as believers, that no matter how much cultural pressure there is (from society or our peers) pushing us toward decisions that dishonor God, when we take a stand for truth—God shows up. We don't always know how or when he will do it, but we can bank on it! When God's people honor God's ways it is always worth it—and the impact is usually greater than we realize.

Such was the case in Daniel chapter 1. And this stand for the truth also enabled Daniel and his friends to be ready for greater future challenges when they would have to take further stands. God often allows his people to be tested. He does so, not to be harsh, but to prepare us for greater feats of spiritual strength. Life is God's training ground. Nothing is random, and nothing is outside of his sovereign view. He sees the stands we take—big and small. And he celebrates each and every one of them.

After passing their initial test with flying colors, we read some extremely powerful words that set the stage for the rest of Daniel's life and the remainder of Daniel's book. In verses 17-21, we read:

> To these four young men God gave knowledge and understanding of all kinds of literature and learning. And Daniel could understand visions and dreams of all kinds. At the end of the time set by the king to bring them into his service, the chief official presented them to Nebuchadnezzar. The king talked with them, and he found none equal to Daniel, Hananiah, Mishael and Azariah; so they entered the king's service. In every matter of wisdom and understanding about which the king questioned them, he found them ten times better than all the magicians and enchanters in his whole kingdom. And Daniel remained there until the first year of King Cyrus.

This test of their faith resulted in them being entrusted with great knowledge and understanding. They aced their Babylonian college courses. They were straight-A students. The culmination of their three-year University of Babylon training was a final oral exam given by the king himself. God was preparing Daniel and his friends to be used in the very place where they had been taken captive. He was in the process of turning their misery into ministry.

In addition to the academic and professional success, Daniel became a prophet—having been given the ability to understand visions and dreams. God gave Daniel supernatural insight because of his courageous obedience. We'll unpack this in greater detail as we work our way through the book of Daniel. The straightforward statement in Daniel 1:17 about Daniel understanding visions and dreams carries far more weight than one might expect from reading that simple phrase.

Furthermore, the king himself noted Daniel's exceptionalness. Even a mighty pagan conqueror took notice that Daniel's life was different and reacted to it. Nonbelievers can be impacted by a godly person. When we serve God faithfully, we become appealing to others and God works behind the scenes in unexpected ways. This truth is noted in Proverbs 16:7, where we read, "When the LORD takes pleasure in anyone's way, he causes their enemies to make peace with them."

So, as a result of this initial moral and spiritual choice made by Daniel and his friends, the four of them eventually entered the king's service, and furthermore, were bumped to the front of the line and placed on top of the heap. The final statement in chapter 1 carries immense weight. Daniel remained in the king's court longer than Nebuchadnezzar himself! Cyrus was a king who much later followed Nebuchadnezzar, after defeating Nebuchadnezzar's successors. The Lord can bless his own in ways that outlast and even outlive the worldly rulers who seem invincible. The godly teenager who took a bold stand of leadership to honor his God wound up having more longevity than the man he served—the king of the greatest superpower of the day! You will see that as we work our way through the book of Daniel, God's sovereignty will shine brighter and brighter with each chapter.

The Hero's Next Step

Daniel chapter 1 ends with somewhat of a resolution. Daniel's immense success led to him being known and promoted by the king of Babylon. All seems calm and settled—until the opening verse of chapter 2. As we begin reading chapter 2, we catch a glimpse of what God was preparing Daniel for next. It opens with the next plot point—Nebuchadnezzar's terrible night of dreams. God was at work, setting up Daniel for the next step in his unique journey.

The king followed his normal pattern of consulting anyone and everyone in his kingdom whom he thought might be able to shed some light on his nightmare. Magicians, enchanters, sorcerers, and astrologers were the telephone psychics of the day—the snake oil salesmen who dabbled in the occult. They were the people the king normally turned to in an attempt to gain an understanding of mysterious, otherworldly matters. Yet the king was savvy enough to know they were ultimately charlatans. In Daniel 2:5-6,

NEBUCHADNEZZAR
(A.K.A. NEBBY)

we read, "The king replied to the astrologers, 'This is what I have firmly decided: If you do not tell me what my dream was and interpret it, I will have you cut into pieces and your houses turned into piles of rubble. But if you tell me the dream and explain it, you will receive from me gifts and rewards and great honor. So tell me the dream and interpret it for me.'"

The king laid down the gauntlet. Come through for me and you'll be rewarded richly. Fail, and you will die. After the frauds' repeated attempts to convince Nebuchadnezzar that he should tell them about his dream before its interpretation, the king had had enough; and in verse 12, he ordered the execution of "all the wise men of Babylon." As the commander of the king's guard was in the process of executing the king's order, Daniel intervened. Daniel asked to be told the basic information related to the situation, took a deep breath, and then went to the king. Once again, God was sovereignly working behind the scenes and the hero of our story was at a crossroads as he faced an even greater test of faith.

Daniel put his own life on the line by asking the king for more time to interpret the dream. This was not a slam dunk. Daniel knew nothing about the dream, but he went back to his three faithful friends and asked them to pray. If God didn't come through, then they would all be dead, along with the rest of the wise men (verse 18).

Once again, God came through for Daniel and his friends and honored their righteous step of faith. God revealed the dream's meaning to Daniel in a vision (verse 19). Notice the kingdom theme and the focus on God's sovereignty in Daniel's response! In Daniel 2:20-23, we read this incredible prayer of thanks and praise:

Praise be to the name of God for ever and ever; wisdom and
  power are his.
He changes times and seasons; he deposes kings and raises up
  others.
He gives wisdom to the wise and knowledge to the discerning.
He reveals deep and hidden things; he knows what lies in
  darkness, and light dwells with him.
I thank and praise you, God of my ancestors:
You have given me wisdom and power, you have made known
  to me what we asked of you, you have made known to us the
  dream of the king.

Then Daniel shares the details and the interpretation of the sweeping prophetic dream with Nebuchadnezzar and blows the king's mind. His dream featured a large statue with a golden head and various less-valuable metals that made up the rest of the body. The main takeaway for Nebuchadnezzar was that he, and his kingdom (the golden head), would be short-lived with an impending expiration date. (We'll discuss this prophecy in chapter 8. It is the broadest prophetic sweep of world history that the Lord gave to any of the Old Testament prophets!)

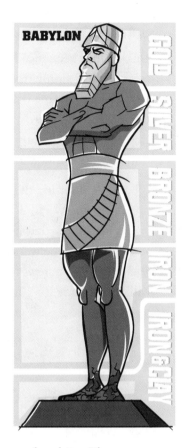

Now picture this scene…and when you do, remind yourself that just one chapter prior, Daniel was a scared teenager, captive in a foreign land with no connections except for his three fellow captive friends from Judah. God had prepared him once again—for an even greater moment.

Pay attention to the actions and words of the king. In Daniel 2:46-49, we read:

> Then King Nebuchadnezzar fell prostrate before Daniel and paid him honor and ordered that an offering and incense be presented to him. The king said to Daniel, "Surely your God is the God of gods and the Lord of kings and a revealer of mysteries, for you were able to reveal this mystery." Then the king placed Daniel in a high position and lavished many gifts on him. He made him ruler over the entire province of Babylon and placed him in charge of all its wise men. Moreover, at Daniel's request the king appointed Shadrach, Meshach and Abednego administrators over the province of Babylon, while Daniel himself remained at the royal court.

Because of the commitment Daniel lived out to the Lord during the events of chapter 1, the prophet had the faith necessary and was able to save the lives of many people (including his own) in Daniel chapter 2.

Setting the Stage

This opening sequence in the book of Daniel sets the stage for the rest of the book. Daniel simply took on one trial at a time and honored God the best he could during his Babylonian training. Each time, God blessed Daniel's faithfulness and entrusted him and his friends with more and more. At each step in Daniel's early journey in Babylon, God prepared Daniel for something bigger and better.

What is God setting the stage for in your life right now? What test of faith is on your path? What tension exists where you can place trust in God's sovereignty and know that he is currently working behind the scenes to position you right where he wants you? "Jesus Christ is the same yesterday and today and forever" (Hebrews 13:8). If you have called upon him as your Savior, God will do the same for you. Choose his ways today. You just may be surprised by what he does with you tomorrow. You were called for such a time as this!

Friends in the Fiery Furnace

If we are thrown into the blazing furnace, the God we serve is able to deliver us from it, and he will deliver us from Your Majesty's hand. But even if he does not, we want you to know, Your Majesty, that we will not serve your gods or worship the image of gold you have set up.

DANIEL 3:17-18

We are here.

DANIEL

1 2 3 4 5 6 7 8 9 10 11 12

HISTORICAL NARRATIVE   PREDICTIVE PROPHECY

The sun was blazing on the vast Mesopotamian desert plain. The crowd was larger than any they had ever seen. They stood shoulder to shoulder, crammed in by the large mass of humanity, knowing that a life-or-death decision was about to be made. As the strange and unfamiliar Babylonian music began to play, like the ripple effect caused by a drop of water into a pond, the people closest to the pagan orchestra bowed first. Then as the surrounding sea of people followed the wave of bowing postures, it headed right toward Shadrach, Meshach, and Abednego—and it was decision time.

As the giant ten-story statue glistened in the sun—nearly blinding anyone who gazed upon it for more than a moment—time seemed to slow down as the throng of worshippers surrounding the three young Hebrew men flattened their bodies to the ground in the direction toward the giant idol.

As the wave of low-lying worshippers passed the three of them, they looked at one another—hoping that none of the other two had caved in, and they were all still standing in unison against the ordinance of an idol-worshipping king who had demanded their obedience.

The three men stood tall on the vast plain—now covered with countless bodies bowing low. The three defiant Hebrews may as well have been ten feet tall. There was nowhere to hide from those around them, and their disobedience was reported to the king. Only God knew what would happen next. But the three courageous men placed their fate into the hands of their God—come death or deliverance. Now, there was no turning back.

The Babylonian Idol

If you want to trace the themes of good and evil in the Bible, one way is to follow the histories of Jerusalem and Babylon. Jerusalem is called the city of God. Babylon, on the other hand, has a rebellious and evil beginning, with the tower of Babel, and this theme carries through all of Scripture—culminating in Revelation 17 and 18, where we read about its future destruction. Babylon is both a place and a system, similar to how we refer to Wall Street, which is both a literal location and, at the same time, represents the whole financial system that takes place there.

Babylon appears in two key forms in the Old Testament. First, in a man-centered, God-defying religious form, seen in the account of Nimrod and the Tower of Babel (Genesis 11). Second, around 1,650 years later we read about Babylon again, this time in a wealthy, conquering political form under Nebuchadnezzar. Polytheism and idol worship were inherent to the Babylonian system, and to all of the surrounding nations, for that matter. Later, idol worship was the key element that caused the downfall of both Israel and Judah.

We end Daniel chapter 2 with Nebuchadnezzar acknowledging the majesty of the Lord to Daniel. In verse 47, Daniel records the king saying, "Surely your God is the God of gods and the Lord of kings and a revealer of mysteries." But like many a world leader, the king's humility was short lived. Whether it was the polytheism of the Babylonian culture that allowed Nebuchadnezzar to view the Lord as one of many gods, or the pride of the king's heart, hardened after only a momentary realization that Daniel's God was altogether different, we don't know.

In any case, the bottom line is that Nebuchadnezzar doubled down on his pride and built a pagan idol that everyone was required to bow down to and worship. Much like the forced assimilation Daniel and the other exiles experienced, this pagan and political rite was designed to unify the Babylonian Empire under the king. Evil despots always clamor for total submission and complete control of the masses.

The statue was roughly 90 feet high and nine feet wide. Using biblical measurements, the original text in Daniel 3 measures the statue at "sixty cubits high and six cubits wide" (verse 1). It makes sense for the king to have patterned this giant idol after the statue in his dream, but with one significant detail changed. The entire statue was made of gold. All Babylon. The statue was likely made in the likeness of the king.

In Daniel's interpretation of the king's dream, the prophet spoke a phrase that shook Nebuchadnezzar to his core: "After you, another kingdom will arise" (Daniel 2:39). Those words got under the king's skin. In building his statue, Nebuchadnezzar was metaphorically shaking his fist at God and saying, *I'm not a temporary golden head. I am permanent. No kingdom will conquer Babylon. I am the god of my age. There is no, "after me."*

At the end of the Bible, we discover an interesting parallel in Revelation 13, when people will be forced to take the mark of the beast and worship the image of the antichrist. The Babylonians were a polytheistic people, but it appears that Nebuchadnezzar was essentially announcing, "Worship whatever gods you like, but your ultimate allegiance is to me and my kingdom, or you will die." This is much the same tact that the future antichrist will take when, at the midpoint of the future tribulation period, he will demand allegiance and worship from everyone (by having them take his mark on their right hand or forehead), or they will face death.

Here is the official decree as recorded in Daniel 3:4-6:

> Then the herald loudly proclaimed, "Nations and peoples of every language, this is what you are commanded to do: As soon as you hear the sound of the horn, flute, zither, lyre, harp, pipe and all kinds of music, you must fall down and worship the image of gold

that King Nebuchadnezzar has set up. Whoever does not fall down and worship will immediately be thrown into a blazing furnace."

King Nebuchadnezzar's demand to worship or be put to death is similar to what the antichrist will do. People will be told to bow down. Worship. And take the mark. You can see through these two events—that are thousands of years apart—that the same evil one is behind the forced worship that is being commanded. History marches on, but evil remains the same—until God's future appointed time, when he will set all accounts straight and punish evil once and for all. Until then, wicked rulers will continue to proliferate—backed by the evil entities in the unseen realm.

From Boot Camp to Specialist Training

Apparently, Daniel was not at this gathering. Daniel chapter 2 ends with the prophet's promotion to a high position, where he remained at the royal court (verses 48-49). Because the idol incident was at a different location, the plain of Dura (3:1), Daniel was not there.

Daniel and his friends (referred to in Daniel 3 by their new Babylonian names) Shadrach, Meshach, and Abednego, had remained faithful to the Lord through their boot camp in chapters 1 and 2. They passed the tests and prospered, even in the face of hardship. Now came their specialist training.

As we can relate to in our current age, evil will always rear its ugly head again and again—usually with multiplied ferocity, like the mythological Greek monster Hydra. For Shadrach, Meshach, and Abednego, previously this meant that the three Hebrew teens had to eat vegetables and pray for God to help Daniel interpret a dream. These were risky actions that could have resulted in their deaths if God hadn't showed up, but these were minor tests compared to what they faced now in Daniel chapter 3.

Imagine the scene. The three friends were separated from their newfound leader Daniel, and they were standing in a sea of people—that included Babylon's myriad of officials—all of whom were bowing down to Nebuchadnezzar's idolatrous golden statue. The three friends were employed by the king (2:49), yet they were the only three who stood defiantly tall rather than bowing to the giant pagan lump of metal. Once again, they passed an even greater test. This didn't take place in a back room or a prayer closet, but out in the open—in front of the king, for all the world to see. This time, there was no way out—but God had something even better in store.

Calling them out for their defiance, Nebuchadnezzar asked them, "What god will be able to rescue you from my hand?" (verse 15). I love the unified response from Shadrach, Meshach, and Abednego. We read these powerful and faith-filled words in Daniel 3:16-18:

King Nebuchadnezzar, we do not need to defend ourselves before you in this matter. If we are thrown into the blazing furnace, the God we serve is able to deliver us from it, and he will deliver us from Your Majesty's hand. But even if he does not, we want you to know, Your Majesty, that we will not serve your gods or worship the image of gold you have set up.

We know the outcome of the story, but in that moment, the three courageous young men did not. The phrase "the God we serve is able to deliver us" was followed by "but even if he does not." That is faith in action. It reminds us of the words of Job, who said, "Though he slay me, yet will I hope in him" (Job 13:15).

The furious king ordered that the furnace be heated to seven times hotter than was standard (Daniel 3:19). He had the three defiant Hebrews tied up tight, then thrown into the fire. So hot was the fire that it killed those who threw the three friends into the furnace (3:22)!

But then something amazing happened. The king had to double-check his math when he saw four men walking around in the fire. What the king said next (verse 25) should blow our minds. There, we read, "Look! I see four men walking around in the fire, unbound and unharmed, and the fourth looks like a son of the gods."

He was right and wrong. There were four men walking around. But the fourth was not a son of the gods, it was the Son of God! This preincarnate (before the first coming) appearance of Jesus in the Old Testament is a thing of absolute beauty and mystery. Theologians differ on whether the fourth being was in fact an angel, the Angel of the Lord, or a preincarnate appearance of Christ. Personally, I believe the Angel of the Lord who shows up a few times

throughout the Old Testament is the preincarnate Christ, and I believe this fourth man here in Daniel 3 was Jesus walking with the three Hebrew men in the fire.

By the way, men don't walk around in fires. They suffocate. They burn up. So, Nebuchadnezzar and all of those watching personally witnessed two miracles happening at once. They saw men alive and walking around among intense flames, and on top of that, an additional being was present in the fire with the three men. The text then informs us that Shadrach, Meshach, and Abednego emerged from the fire without even smelling like smoke. The only things that had burned were the ropes that had bound them!

We can take away many practical lessons from this account. One is that when God's people go through fiery trials formed by the enemy, the only things that will be truly destroyed are the things that bind them. God often allows trials in our life to free us from our reliance on the worldly things that tie us up. Romans 8:28 tells us plainly that "we know that in all things God works for the good of those who love him, who have been called according to his purpose."

Also, as followers of Christ, we are to be in the world but not of it (see John 17:14). We must remember that earth is not our home. Though the flames are all around us, we can emerge without the smell of fire. Though we are sinners living in a sinful world, Jesus paid it all and the Father sees those of us who have put our trust in Christ as sinless—without even a whiff of smoke on our clothes. We don't have to become jaded, depressed, lustful, angry, or hopeless in response to the sinful struggles around us. We are called to be different. We can be different.

That doesn't mean we are immune to death or sickness or hardship or trials. But God will use all for our good and his glory. In the end, every fiery furnace of life will be shown to have prepared us for eternity with the Lord. The Bible teaches that salvation is free—paid for by Christ on the cross. But it also teaches that we will be given eternal rewards (Romans 14:10-12; 2 Corinthians 5:10) based on how we served our God and how we weathered the storms of life without caving in to temptation.

God's Patience

Once again, God draws Nebuchadnezzar toward a relationship with himself. In the closing verses of Daniel 3, the king is found praising God once again. Yet there is an indication that Nebuchadnezzar still sees the God of Daniel and his friends as one of many gods (see verse 28).

It seems the king was in awe of God as one of many lesser gods. He still didn't get it. He was being drawn by the one true God— the creator of all things seen and unseen.

The Babylonians worshipped fire as homage to their sun god. So, the survival of Shadrach, Meshach, and Abednego served as an object lesson to the king and the Babylonians that the sun god had failed. He was lesser. In fact, their sun god was no god at all. That was the point God was making.

In an ironic move, Nebuchadnezzar shifts from threatening to kill anyone who doesn't worship his statue to threatening to kill anyone who says "anything against the God of Shadrach, Meshach, and Abednego" (verse 29). The king concludes his new threat with another indication that he is still polytheistic, as noted by the phrase "for no other god can save in this way." Instead, he should have said, "There is no other god but the one true God." The king of Babylon had missed the point—again.

The chapter ends with one final sentence mentioning the fact that the king promoted the three fiery-furnace survivors to yet other higher positions in his kingdom. As much as the enemy works from the unseen realm to defeat God's people, Satan's efforts will ultimately come up short and God will always use the evil intentions for the benefit of the people of God—either in this life or when we cross the veil into God's presence. We have nothing to fear.

Prophetic Foreshadows

If you will recall, I stated that the book of Daniel is split into six chapters of historical narrative and six chapters of prophecy, but that the narrative sections contain prophecy, and vice versa. Chapters 2 and 3 of Daniel serve as a case in point. In chapter 2, we read the narrative of the events surrounding the king's dream and the prophetic interpretation of the dream (which we'll cover in chapter 8, when we shift our focus to the prophetic sections of Daniel). Here in chapter 3, it's all narrative, yet there are several prophetic types or foreshadows that become apparent once one studies the entire Bible.

In relation to the mark of the beast connection I cited above, there is another foreshadow of end-times events found in Daniel 3. During the future tribulation period, most people will take the mark of the beast so that they aren't killed. But there will also be a small group of people that experience a different outcome.

When you put all of the prophetic puzzle pieces together, you discover that a remnant of the Jewish people will refuse the mark of the beast and still survive. They will be supernaturally protected by God in Bozrah/Petra and will eventually realize Jesus was their promised Messiah after all. Then they will corporately call upon the name of Jesus (see Isaiah 63:1; Zechariah 12:10; 13:7-9; Matthew 23:39; Romans 11:25-27; Revelation 12:14). This remnant of Jewish people will walk through the fiery furnace of the trials of the tribulation period and, in the end, will be united with the Lord.

We'll wade through a lot more prophecy in some upcoming chapters, but I felt it was important to highlight some of the noticeable prophetic foreshadows that are part of Daniel chapter 3. Next, let's look at how God reveals himself in Daniel chapter 4.

CHAPTER 5

Nebby Goes Nutty

Your kingdom will be restored to you when you acknowledge that Heaven rules.

DANIEL 4:26

We are here.

DANIEL

1 2 3 4 5 6 7 8 9 10 11 12

HISTORICAL NARRATIVE   PREDICTIVE PROPHECY

If you'll recall the kingdom context I wrote about in chapter 1—the masterful juxtaposition of the Gentile kingdoms of the world in comparison to the kingdom of God—you'll note the undertones of that theme are present as we take a look at Daniel chapter 4.

Through the events of chapters 2 and 3, God was busy showing Nebuchadnezzar that the God of Daniel and his three friends is the one true God. He was also busy demonstrating that the kingdom of God is the one true and eternal kingdom. Through Nebuchadnezzar's dream in Daniel chapter 2 (which we'll highlight in chapter 8), and through the mysterious man in the fiery furnace, who protected the Hebrew heroes in Daniel chapter 3, God was slowly unveiling his plans for the Jewish people and their connection to God's kingdom.

In short, God is sovereign over kings and kingdoms. Nebuchadnezzar was the leader of the first in a series of Gentile empires that would span history, all the way from Daniel's time until the end times, when God will usher in his kingdom, triumphing over all earthly kings and kingdoms. As the head of the statue representing Gentile kingdoms in Daniel chapter 2, Nebuchadnezzar typifies or symbolizes all Gentile kingdoms. He was a literal king over a literal kingdom, and he is used as an object lesson to juxtapose the kingdoms of the world with the kingdom of God.

In Daniel 4, Nebuchadnezzar—who had already recognized the superior nature of Daniel's God, yet still only revered God as one of many lesser gods—had another encounter with God through yet another dream. The events of chapter 4 occur many years after the events of chapter 3, probably toward the end of Nebuchadnezzar's 43-year reign (605–562 BC). By this time, the king had finished his impressive building projects (verse 30). One of these projects may have been the famous Hanging Gardens of Babylon—one of the Seven Wonders of the ancient world (although not mentioned here in the text of Daniel's book). Daniel would probably have been roughly fifty years old at this point.

The chapter is essentially written as a declaration by the king. Daniel likely copied the official decree into his record, accurately capturing the king's firsthand account. It's not 100 percent clear from the text whether Nebuchadnezzar was ever truly a believer in God as the one true God, but several details in this chapter seem to indicate that he still saw Daniel's God as one of many gods. Superior to others, but in a pantheon of other lesser gods nonetheless. If that is the case, then this chapter is unique in that it is the only chapter in Scripture composed by a nonbeliever—and a pagan polytheist at that.

QUICK FACT: DID YOU KNOW...

that the king's dream in Daniel 4 was patterned after the Gilgamesh Epic—a famous poetic work that dates from between 2150–1400 BC?

Once again, Daniel is called upon to interpret the king's dream. In verse 9, the king refers to Daniel as "chief of the magicians." This does not necessarily mean Daniel was chief over all the wise men, but it could mean that he was the best of the best. His prophetic interpretations always proved true.

QUICK FACT: DID YOU KNOW...

that the Magi from the East in Matthew chapter 2 were very likely connected to the Magi from Daniel's day, more than 500 years before the birth of Christ? *More on this in chapter 13, where we'll study the 70 "weeks" prophecy.*

In Daniel 4:10-12, we read these words recorded by king Nebuchadnezzar himself:

> These are the visions I saw while lying in bed: I looked, and there before me stood a tree in the middle of the land. Its height was enormous. The tree grew large and strong and its top touched the sky; it was visible to the ends of the earth. Its leaves were beautiful, its fruit abundant, and on it was food for all. Under it the wild animals found shelter, and the birds lived in its branches; from it every creature was fed.

Then the king goes on to explain that he saw a holy messenger come down from heaven, commanding that the tree be cut down all the way to the roots. The stump and roots "bound with iron and bronze" were to remain (verse 15). Then, the tree is personified as a man who would lose his mind and live like an animal for a period of time.

Daniel—troubled by having to deliver the news of the dream's meaning—is encouraged by the king to follow through with interpreting the message. He then tells the king, "You are that tree!" (verse 22). Daniel goes on to inform Nebuchadnezzar that the king himself will be driven away from human society, left to live in the wilderness as an animal until "seven times" pass over him (verse 25). Most scholars agree that the context present in Daniel chapter 4 would mean that the period of time being referred to in the dream would be seven years—enough time for his hair and nails to grow out to the lengths described later on in verse 33.

As hard as it was to deliver the interpretation, it did not contain solely bad news. Daniel shared with the king that his kingdom would be restored when he will "acknowledge that Heaven rules" (verse 26). It is unclear if this passage means that the Lord would require Nebuchadnezzar to become a true believer in the one and only God, or merely that the king would be humbled to the point where he recognized God's sovereign rule over everything.

In addition, Daniel even communicated a way for the king to avoid the fulfillment of the prophecy altogether. He called on the king to repent. To renounce his sins and wickedness by behaving rightly and showing kindness to the oppressed. How's that for a straight shooter? Daniel—much like John the Baptist, roughly six centuries later—pointed out the specific sins of the king, and bluntly called him out.

Just a practical side note here. Humans can't sugarcoat sin or deny truth. This practice is destructive and deadly. We understand this in the realm of physical health, but we often miss this when it comes to spiritual health. If someone has cancer, there is no way to avoid telling the patient. Treatment cannot be addressed unless the cancer is identified and acknowledged. Similarly, people can't come to a saving knowledge of Christ unless they see their need for a Savior—until they see their sin for what it is. Before someone gets saved, they need to realize what they are getting saved from.

One more practical side note. Notice that Daniel called out Nebuchadnezzar's sin within the context of an existing relationship and a crisis of belief. Context and timing are everything—and our approach must be Spirit led. We can't change culture by cursing the darkness. Darkness is going to be dark. Instead, we must leverage Spirit-led opportunities to lead individuals to the light—to Christ. Cultures and societies can't be saved. Only individuals can.

Now, back to our regularly scheduled chapter. As we'll see later in the prophetic chapters of Daniel's book, there is often a developmental, stage-setting period that lies between a prophecy and its fulfillment. Such was the case here. We read this in Daniel 4:29-33:

> Twelve months later, as the king was walking on the roof of the royal palace of Babylon, he said, "Is not this the great Babylon I have built as the royal residence, by my mighty power and for the glory of my majesty?" Even as the words were on his lips, a voice came from heaven, "This is what is decreed for you, King Nebuchadnezzar: Your royal authority has been taken from you. You will be driven away from people and will live with the wild animals;

you will eat grass like the ox. Seven times will pass by for you until you acknowledge that the Most High is sovereign over all kingdoms on earth and gives them to anyone he wishes." Immediately what had been said about Nebuchadnezzar was fulfilled.

God executed his judgment exactly in the way he said that he would and applied it in full. Nebuchadnezzar lost control of his kingdom and was in the wild for "seven times."

And then King Nebuchadnezzar says this to the nations and peoples of the earth at the culmination of his experience— remember, Daniel chapter 4 is a decree from the king:

> At the end of that time, I, Nebuchadnezzar, raised my eyes toward heaven, and my sanity was restored. Then I praised the Most High; I honored and glorified him who lives forever. His dominion is an eternal dominion; his kingdom endures from generation to generation (verse 34).

The king's intent for this proclamation was for everyone in all kingdoms to know and understand what the most high God could do, even to the person who was considered the greatest on earth. A few verses later, the ancient ruler ended his declaration with this powerful statement: "Now I, Nebuchadnezzar, praise and exalt and glorify the King of heaven, because everything he does is right and all his ways are just. And those who walk in pride he is able to humble" (verse 37).

Nebuchadnezzar's pride was his downfall. The Lord humbled him as an example for everyone. Pride is the root of all sin. It is what led to Lucifer's rebellion (Isaiah 14:12-14; Ezekiel 28:17; 1 Timothy 3:6), Adam and Eve's rebellion (Genesis 3), and is indeed what has led to every rebellion since (1 John 2:16). God showed the representative of all worldly kingdoms that he alone is sovereign—the one true King of kings and Lord of lords.

Missing Heaven by 18 Inches

As detailed above, it is not completely clear whether Nebuchadnezzar actually became a believer. But it is clear the Lord gave him every opportunity—including humbling him for seven years to really get his attention!

When we get to heaven, I imagine we may be surprised to see some people there whom we didn't expect to see. I also think that we may be surprised by who are missing, whom we thought would be there.

To be clear, salvation is obtained only through a relationship with Jesus Christ. We can't do enough good deeds to enter heaven based on our own merits. It's only through the blood of Christ that we can be forgiven. My point here is that people can miss heaven by 18 inches. That is roughly the distance between our heads and our hearts.

Many people have gained some head knowledge about God. They may have sensed God working in their lives in an attempt to draw them to the Savior. Perhaps they even go to church. But only God knows the heart. When I view the total context of Nebuchadnezzar's story, I tend to think that this was the case with the ancient king. He acknowledged God, but he seemed to have clung to his polytheism. He viewed "Daniel's God" as the most powerful god, but one of many. It seems to me that Nebuchadnezzar may have given God mental assent, but he never surrendered his life to God. The Lord never became "Nebuchadnezzar's God."

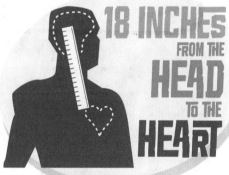

Viewing the book of Daniel from a New Testament (John 3:16) perspective, you might say that Nebuchadnezzar realized that "God so loved the world," but the king never became one of the *whosoevers* who would come to a personal saving faith in the Lord.

What about you? Do you know *about* the Lord, or do you *know* the Lord? Have you placed your trust in the one who died for your sins? If not, why not nail that down today? Read the following world-famous verse and put your name in place of "whoever."

> *For God so loved the world that he gave his one and only Son, that whoever believes in him shall not perish but have eternal life* (John 3:16).

Be sure that you don't miss heaven by 18 inches!

CHAPTER 6

Belshazzar's Big Mistake

Suddenly the fingers of a human hand appeared and wrote on the plaster of the wall, near the lampstand in the royal palace.

DANIEL 5:5

We are here.

DANIEL

1 2 3 4 5 6 7 8 9 10 11 12

HISTORICAL NARRATIVE   PREDICTIVE PROPHECY

If you are a fan of the Indiana Jones movies, you'll appreciate the archeological facts I'm about to share. In the 1800s, researchers, explorers, and educators from the West began to embark on various archeological digs throughout the Middle East. Many discoveries of ancient artifacts were made during this time, but one in particular helped to shed light on key details from Old Testament history, including the time period of the prophets. Several details in the book of Daniel were clarified and verified through the discovery of the Babylonian Chronicles.

The Babylonian Chronicles are ancient tablets of Babylonian records. Of the known chronicles, several were discovered during this nineteenth-century

archeological boom. Translation of the tablets began in 1887 and continued through 1956. Among the chronicles that have survived (perhaps by sovereign design) are clay tablets that document the dates and historical details of key figures and events that are also recorded in the book of Daniel.

Some of these extrabiblical (outside of the Bible) records verify dates and milestones about the reign of Nebuchadnezzar, as well as record the fall of the Babylonian Empire to the Persian king Cyrus, culminated by the taking of Babylon beginning on Saturday, October 12, 539 BC.[2]

The discovery and translation of the Babylonian Chronicles obliterated the arguments of critics who scoffed at the historical record of the book of Daniel. The archeological discovery vetted key details of Daniel's record, but that still didn't stop critics from continuing to doubt the validity of the prophecies in Daniel. We'll discuss this in detail in chapter 9, but the prophecies of Daniel proved to be so accurate that critics claimed the book had to have been written after the fact—until yet another archeological discovery (perhaps the greatest of all time) proved the critics wrong once again.

It seems that with every turn of the spade in the sands, caves, ruins, and tombs of the Middle East, the biblical record is verified as wholly accurate. These aren't solely small, single-artifact findings (of which there are many), but include momentous, game-changing discoveries like the ancient Hittite library, the Babylonian Chronicles, and the Dead Sea Scrolls, to name a few.

The Christian faith is supported by facts. It is not a blind leap, but a reasonable faith. We cannot see God and we must trust that his Word is true as it relates to our origins, our destiny, the unseen realm, heaven, and many other things. But our faith is built on verifiably accurate facts when it comes to history and science. God has provided a trail of evidence for us to follow. The biblical record has been verified at every turn and fulfilled prophecy is the Bible's built-in proof of authenticity.

The Rise and Fall of Empires

We end Daniel chapter 4 with Nebuchadnezzar humbling himself before God and having his kingdom restored to him. Then we open Daniel chapter 5 with a Babylonian king named Belshazzar ruling with pride and arrogance. So, just to give you an idea of how much time had passed in Daniel's narrative, chapter 5 occurs around 40 years after Nebuchadnezzar returned to his throne.

Belshazzar was coregent (coruler) with his father Nabonidus, who left the city of Babylon to be ruled by his son Belshazzar for about ten years (as recorded in the Babylonian Chronicles and other records). The text of Daniel 5 refers to Nebuchadnezzar as Belshazzar's father. This was used more as a patriarchal term because neither the Hebrew, Aramaic, nor Babylonian (Chaldee) languages had a word for grandfather or grandson. Even today, people refer to Abraham as "Father Abraham." We now know that Belshazzar was, in fact, Nebuchadnezzar's grandson.

Chapter 5 of Daniel opens with the ungodly king throwing a massive pagan party for 1,000 of his nobles, his wives, and his concubines. As the wine flowed freely, the king asked for the holy vessels from the Jewish temple to be brought into the party scene. Verses 3 and 4 paint the picture for us:

> They brought in the gold goblets that had been taken from the

temple of God in Jerusalem, and the king and his nobles, his wives and his concubines drank from them. As they drank the wine, they praised the gods of gold and silver, of bronze, iron, wood and stone.

Bad move. Bad timing. At the time when this great banquet was taking place, the entire area surrounding Babylon had already been conquered by the Medes and Persians. Nabonidus had been defeated and fled the area. Belshazzar and his nobles were holed up in the fortified city of Babylon—which had not fallen to an invading army for 1,000 years because of its strong fortifications.[3]

The Greek historian Herodotus described ancient Babylon as follows:[4]

First, a deep, wide moat full of water surrounds it and forms its outer boundary. Next there is a wall 76 feet in width, 304 feet in height...Along the top edge of the wall, they built one-story chambers facing each other, leaving a space about the size of a passageway for a four-horse chariot between each. Around the wall they installed 100 gates all of bronze, including the pillars and the lintels...The city has two districts, for the River Euphrates divides it in half through the middle. This river is large, deep, and swift. The wall on either bank extends down to the river at an angle and from this point turns to form a drywall brick rampart along each bank of the river...While the outer wall is the city's main defense, there is another wall within it extending around the city which is not much weaker...they have built the royal palace, fortified and surrounded by a huge impregnable wall.

HERODOTUS

So, Belshazzar and his fellow partiers seemed to have rest assured in the fortifications and the history of the impenetrable capital. Additionally, perhaps the feast they were enjoying was to reaffirm their commitment to their pagan gods in hopes of continued protection from the invading forces. In any case, what happened next proved to be scarier than being surrounded by the Medo-Persian army.

We read this in verses 4-6:

> As they drank the wine, they praised the gods of gold and silver, of bronze, iron, wood and stone. Suddenly the fingers of a human hand appeared and wrote on the plaster of the wall, near the lamp-stand in the royal palace. The king watched the hand as it wrote. His face turned pale and he was so frightened that his legs became weak and his knees were knocking.

The mysterious writing on the wall from a giant unknown hand struck terror in the heart of the drunken king. He sobered up quickly and summoned his astrologers and magicians to get an explanation.

As was the case in Daniel chapters 2 and 4, none of the pagan psychics of the day could tell Belshazzar what the words meant. However, Daniel—the one true prophet in the kingdom—could. The king offered Daniel riches and position in exchange for the interpretation. I love Daniel's response. In verse 17, he answered the king by saying, "You may keep your gifts for yourself and give your rewards to someone else. Nevertheless, I will read the writing for the king and tell him what it means." What integrity. What focus. What perspective.

QUICK FACT: DID YOU KNOW...

that archeologists discovered a large 56'x173' throne room (the probable location of Belshazzar's feast) in the ruins of Nebuchadnezzar's palace?[5]

Now in his later years (Daniel likely would have been around age 80) and having seen God work in history to fulfill prophecy, the confident Daniel preached a bold sermon to the king. He called Belshazzar out for ignoring what God had done through the humbling of the king's grandfather. Daniel also called him out for defiantly using the goblets from the Lord's temple to honor meaningless gods.

Then the prophet read and interpreted the supernatural writing on the wall in verses 25-28:

> This is the inscription that was written: MENE, MENE, TEKEL, PARSIN. Here is what these words mean: *Mene*: God has numbered the days of your reign and brought it to an end. *Tekel*: You have been weighed on the scales and found wanting. *Peres*: Your kingdom is divided and given to the Medes and Persians.

Belshazzar's fate was sealed. Only two verses later, in the final verses of Daniel chapter 5, we read of God's swift judgment as this prophecy was quickly fulfilled. Verses 30-31 read, "That very night Belshazzar, king of the Babylonians, was slain, and Darius the Mede took over the kingdom, at the age of sixty-two."

We know from ancient historical documents (including those mentioned at the opening of this chapter) that on October 13, 539 BC, the fall of Babylon was complete.[6] The Medo-Persian forces had redirected the Euphrates River, allowing their army to enter the city through the riverbed without any resistance whatsoever. The 1,000-year impenetrable fortress had been breached. Belshazzar had gone too far, inviting God's judgment.

A Warning for Us Today

Notice the generational degeneration from Nebuchadnezzar to Belshazzar. Nebuchadnezzar was prideful and arrogant, but when God's correction came via seven years of living with wild animals, the king recognized God was the one who was really in charge.

Fast-forward several decades, and the empire's new leader had ignored his grandfather's experiences and doubled down on increasingly wicked ways. He wasn't prideful due to his accomplishments. He had none. Rather, he led the empire into overt debauchery and open celebration of intentional wickedness—specifically directed in opposition to the very God that had spared his grandfather.

In the New Testament, Paul captures the pattern of man's downward moral spiral in Romans 1. It begins from knowing there's a God we must worship, progressing to rejecting that God by the worship of created things, moving to casting off all restraint, then to behaving with the natural order of things twisted—resulting in a state of insane upside-down thinking.

Godless nations follow this trajectory. The entire fallen world is currently following this path—and it is leading to God's coming judgment. God's pattern of judgment follows man's moral decline closely. The human decline that played out in the Babylonian Empire is the same pattern Paul detailed in Romans 1, and it is playing out right before our eyes.

ROMANS
CHAPTER
1

Things that were once held dear—even by non-Christians—are being systematically defiled. Morality. Marriage. Gender. Protecting life. Protecting children from destructive and immoral ideologies. All of these have been progressively eroding in the West for decades.

One author puts it this way:

> Have you noticed how in recent years the world has stepped into the "sanctuary" of faith and laid its ruthless hands on some of the things we hold most sacred? Our day has seen this impious sacrilege carried into many other realms, as well. Is God unmindful of this? Will he not visit for such defiance?[7]

Similar to King Belshazzar intentionally disrespecting and corrupting the instruments of God, our current culture seems dead set on defiling what has long been held as sacred. At some point, God will judge such evil. In upcoming chapters in this book, we will learn about a future time when God will do just that—globally.

Lastly, one practical takeaway from Belshazzar's story is that one day we will all give an account. At some point, each person will stand before the Creator. When we do, we will either stand covered in the righteousness of Christ, or we will stand to give an account for our sins and bear their consequences. Thankfully, Jesus already paid for our sins on the cross, and if we receive him as our Savior, God's judgment will pass over us, having already been paid by our Divine Substitute.

In the famous words of the old hymn, "Jesus paid it all, all to him I owe / Sin had left a crimson stain—He washed it white as snow."[8]

CHAPTER 7

Facing Lions

When Daniel learned that the decree had been published, he went home to his upstairs room where the windows opened toward Jerusalem. Three times a day he got down on his knees and prayed, giving thanks to his God, just as he had done before.

DANIEL 6:10

On August 14, 2021, a 7.2-magnitude earthquake shook Haiti, killing at least 1,941 people.[9] As terrible as that was, just over a decade earlier, a 7.0-magnitude quake hit Haiti on January 12, 2010, killing an estimated 40,000–316,000 people (depending on the source), and displaced nearly 1 million people.[10] What accounted for the stark difference in the levels of devastation that were experienced in the same geographic area only 11-and-a-half years apart?

When civil engineers plan and build structures, they do so by studying the stability of what the structure is built upon and understanding the various stresses that the structure will need to endure based on its intended purpose, then they plan accordingly. A structure made only of concrete—while strong enough to withstand its own weight and exposure to the elements of the outdoors such as sun, wind, and rain—will not hold up under a massive earthquake.

An engineering solution has been developed for the construction of concrete buildings by also including rebar (short for reinforcing bars) as a building material. Rebar seems to have been first invented in France around 1850 (patented in 1867), then use of the material in America followed soon after.[11] The metal bars, usually iron or steel, form a skeleton to pour concrete around to give the structure the ability to handle more weight and stress than a building made of only concrete.

Many of the buildings in Haiti are made using concrete. In the 2010 earthquake, a contributing factor to what made the death toll so high was that most of the structures that had collapsed had been constructed without rebar. They had no inner strength. No integrity.

Well, as we've seen since the beginning, Daniel passed each test of his faith and commitment with flying colors. On each occasion, his faith was strengthened. Next, in Daniel chapter 6, the prophet faced an even greater test. But Daniel had built with rebar in his concrete, so to speak. He was a man of integrity. His character had been developed to take on the next big test without cracking under the pressure.

Daniel's life, filled with consistent obedience in the same direction toward the Lord, had prepared and strengthened him for another giant moment in the narrative of the book of Daniel. Let's take a look.

Not Fair!

Each one of us, as a child or teenager, has complained about some situation or outcome not being fair. The older we get, the more we realize that life is not fair. Often, evil people form twisted plots hatched from wicked intentions. Such was the case in Daniel chapter 6. By this time, Daniel was an old man, having lived decades in Babylon and witnessing the transition of empires from the Babylonians to the Medo-Persians. With each transition of leadership, Daniel had garnered favor with the new ruler. Such was the case regarding his relationship with the new king, Darius.

When the Medo-Persians conquered the Babylonians, the Medo-Persian realm became the largest empire in history up to that point. Under Cyrus, three top-tier administrators were put in place to manage large areas of the vast empire. Darius (also known as Gobryas), was one of these administrators. Darius was viewed as a king, and Cyrus—who ruled over the entire empire—referred to himself as the "king of kings." Darius established 120 rulers under him, known as satraps, to help govern the province of Babylon. He also appointed three rulers over the 120 satraps. And Daniel was one of these three rulers.

With Daniel probably in his eighties, having lived most of his life in exile and doing so with incredible integrity, his godly reputation preceded him. Darius held Daniel in high regard and planned to put him in charge of the entire Babylonian province (Daniel 6:3). However, the two other administrators and the satraps did not like this idea.

We're not told the specific reasons that motivated the satraps' actions, but they, with the other administrators, devised a plan to remove Daniel out of the picture. Perhaps Daniel stood in the way of their schemes. People of integrity tend to hold back tides of corruption. Or perhaps they were just jealous of Daniel's favored standing. There may have been antisemitism in play as well because Daniel was specifically referred to as an exile from Judah who "pays no attention" to the king (see Daniel 6:13). Shadrach, Meshach, and Abed-nego faced this same treatment back in Daniel 3:12.

Whatever their reasons, we read telling verses that reveal the satraps' complete lack of integrity and highlight Daniel's consistent practice of the opposite. In Daniel 6:4-5, we read,

> The administrators and the satraps tried to find grounds for charges against Daniel in his conduct of government affairs, but they were unable to do so. They could find no corruption in him, because he was trustworthy and neither corrupt nor negligent. Finally these men said, "We will never find any basis for charges against this man Daniel unless it has something to do with the law of his God."

2 Timothy 3:12—In fact, everyone who wants to live a godly life in Christ Jesus will be persecuted.

What uprightness and commitment, that even corrupt politicians could spot it. What dedication and consistency, that unbelievers would note Daniel's complete commitment to the Lord. Oh, that we who claim the name of Christ would live in such a way!

Recognizing that Daniel followed the laws of his God, the evil and crafty leaders used flattery and fancy talk to execute an intricate plan to trick Darius into proclaiming a statute that no person in the kingdom can pray to any god or human being except for Darius himself for 30 days (Daniel 6:6-7). Initially unconsidered by Darius, this edict would set Daniel's dedication to the Lord on a collision course with the law. Once it was inked, the law could not be revoked. Such was the nature of the laws of that time. Unlike Nebuchadnezzar had in the previous empire, Darius did not have complete autonomy. He was subject to Cyrus and the laws of the Medo-Persian Empire, even to the very law that he himself had put forth. And consequently, Darius had to abide by the law, even if its enforcement placed his friend Daniel's life in danger.

Verse 10 demonstrates that the old prophet did not allow a new external pressure to alter his daily spiritual habits.

The men who were out to get Daniel witnessed him praying and brought this to the attention of King Darius. This grieved the king, and he looked for ways to save Daniel; however, he came up empty. Daniel's path to the den of lions was set.

The details of the text reveal that the lions' den was a large underground area with an entrance at the top, over which a large stone was placed. Daniel was thrown into this pit, and all Darius could do was wait and pray that his friend would somehow survive. Daniel 6:17-20 tells us:

> A stone was brought and placed over the mouth of the den, and the king sealed it with his own signet ring and with the rings of his nobles, so that Daniel's situation might not be changed. Then the king returned to his palace and spent the night without eating and without any entertainment being brought to him. And he could not sleep. At the first light of dawn, the king got up and hurried to the lions' den. When he came near the den, he called to Daniel in an anguished voice, "Daniel, servant of the living God, has your God, whom you serve continually, been able to rescue you from the lions?"

And Daniel answered the king.

One can't help but notice the parallels that are present here with the death, burial, and resurrection of Jesus Christ, whose tomb had a stone placed over it that was sealed by the Romans. Daniel was not resurrected, but the righteous prophet was preserved and he emerged from his would-be tomb. This seems to be a clear Old Testament type that points to the Messiah's victorious emergence from his stone-covered tomb.

There is one more parallel that seems to serve as typology that points to the cross. After Daniel's emergence from the pit, Darius commanded that those who had hatched the plot to kill Daniel would themselves be thrown into the lions' den (verse 24). Satan and his evil minions, acting behind the Jewish religious leaders and the Romans who scourged Jesus and crucified him, were unknowingly sealing their own fate. What Satan viewed as a victory in the death of Jesus was actually his own undoing. The resurrection of Christ three days later sealed Satan's fate. Ultimately, only a little bit of time stands between today and Satan's punishment in Revelation 20:10, when Satan will be thrown into the Lake of Fire.

Humanity's Choice

The structure of the narrative in Daniel chapter 6 mirrors some of the previous chapters, when rulers of the empire witnessed the care and preservation provided by the one true God. Recall Nebuchadnezzar's reaction to the interpretation of his dream (Daniel 2:46-49), his response to the preservation of Daniel's friends through the fiery furnace (3:28-30), and his repentance after losing his mind for seven years (4:34-37). You'll note a similar pattern with Darius.

Upon seeing that Daniel survived the night in the lion's den unscathed, Darius issues a decree that is full of praise for the God of the universe. In Daniel 6:26-27, he proclaims,

> I issue a decree that in every part of my kingdom people must fear and reverence the God of Daniel. For he is the living God and he endures forever; his kingdom will not be destroyed, his dominion will never end. He rescues and he saves; he performs signs and wonders in the heavens and on the earth. He has rescued Daniel from the power of the lions.

Notice the varied responses of each of the kings in the book of Daniel when they were faced with a bold witness by the men from Judah and their sovereign God. Nebuchadnezzar, who seems to have missed heaven by only 18 inches. Darius, who's praise of the Lord seemed to have been genuine and undivided. And between them, Belshazzar, who didn't give any praise or recognition to the Lord, and he died that very night.

When you think about it, these are three types of responses we all can have when encountering the Savior. You can give mental assent but refuse to go all in and give the Lord your heart. You can completely neglect to acknowledge the Lord at all and adopt a humanistic pleasure-seeking approach to life. Or you can recognize the one true Lord and enter a true relationship with him through the cross of Christ. The choice is yours. Let's not choose like Nebuchadnezzar or Belshazzar. Instead, let us respond like Darius and praise the living God. Then, let's follow the Lord like Daniel did and live committed lives that are built with integrity.

SECTION 2:

FULFILLED PROPHECY

SECTION 1: HIS-STORY	SECTION 2: FULFILLED PROPHECY	SECTION 3: YET-FUTURE PROPHECY	SECTION 4: APPLICATION

If you have read some of my other books or have heard me speak, you may remember that what brought me to the point of believing that the Bible was from God, helping lead me to Christ, were the facts surrounding fulfilled Bible prophecy. When I pondered the clear fulfillments of prophecies about Christ's first coming, as well as some other Old Testament prophecies that clearly came to pass, it got my attention.

A FEW EXAMPLES OF WORLD EVENTS PROPHESIED IN SCRIPTURE

...AND FULFILLED IN HISTORY!

FOUR EMPIRES: BABYLON, MEDO-PERSIA, GREECE, ROME	DANIEL CH. 2, 7
DESTRUCTION OF THE CITY OF TYRE	EZEKIEL 26
DESTRUCTION OF THE CITY OF SIDON	EZEKIEL 28
PERSIAN KING CYRUS PROPHESIED BY NAME	ISAIAH 44-45
JEWISH PEOPLE WOULD BE DISPERSED 2X'S	ISAIAH 11:11
ISRAEL WOULD BE REBORN IN A DAY AFTER A LONG TIME	ISAIAH 66:8

Fulfilled prophecy is one of the strongest types of evidence that the Bible truly is from God. But one must take the time to look at and evaluate it. Working like a good detective or journalist, one must do the hard (but rewarding) tasks of gathering facts and comparing data for themselves. Only then can fulfilled Bible prophecy leave such a deep impression on a person's convictions regarding the reliability and divine nature of the Bible. It has the power to both convince skeptics and strengthen the faith of believers. Either the Bible is from God, or it is not. Fulfilled prophecy stands as an authoritative testimony that it is. It is evidence that helps demonstrate that the Bible is God's Word, without error, and has been faithfully preserved through history.

As we dive into Section 2, we'll focus much more on the prophecies that are in the book of Daniel, specifically in Daniel chapters 7–12. As we do, keep in mind that these prophecies were given during the time span that is covered by Daniel chapters 1–6. Picture in your mind where the contents of chapters 7–12 are dropped into the timeline of chapters 1–6. I'll point out some relevant dates and the chronology as needed, but I want to reiterate that, at this point in Daniel's book, there is a significant shift of focus from historical narrative to prophecy. As always, context is key. Now, with a better understanding of the narrative sections of Daniel, we will pivot to the incredible and far-reaching prophecies that are found in his book.

Statues and Beasts

The sovereignty, power and greatness of all the kingdoms under heaven will be handed over to the holy people of the Most High. His kingdom will be an everlasting kingdom, and all rulers will worship and obey him.

DANIEL 7:27

We are here.

DANIEL

1 2 3 4 5 6 7 8 9 10 11 12

HISTORICAL NARRATIVE   PREDICTIVE PROPHECY

We have discussed how the book of Daniel is written both as narrative and prophecy. Now, we will also look at a different literary attribute of the book in more detail. Daniel's incredible record is written in two languages, Aramaic and Hebrew. The Aramaic sections were written for a Gentile (non-Jewish) audience and the Hebrew sections were written for a Jewish audience.

Daniel 2:4b through 7:28 were written in Aramaic. This aligns with the intended audience and the subject of the content: information related to the history and future of Gentile kingdoms. Remember the kingdom theme we discussed? The language these passages were written in supports the effort to communicate an important message to the kingdoms it concerned. There are specific detailed prophecies, both concerning Jews and Gentiles, that span from Daniel's time all the way to the last days. In this chapter, we'll look at the sweeping Gentile prophecies found in Daniel chapters 2 and 7.

In the New Testament, Jesus tells us that even in the last days "Jerusalem will be trampled underfoot by the Gentiles, until the times of the Gentiles are fulfilled" (Luke 21:24 ESV). As we'll see in the following prophecies, the times of the Gentiles began when Nebuchadnezzar conquered Jerusalem in 605 BC and will continue until God sets up his future millennial kingdom. If that sounds strange to you, don't let it throw you. We're about to unpack it all as we study the prophecies of Daniel chapters 2 and 7 together.

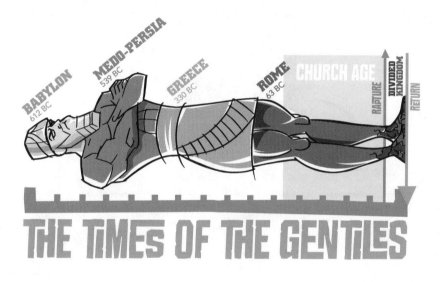

THE TIMES OF THE GENTILES

In chapter 3 of this book, when we discussed Nebuchadnezzar's mysterious statue dream that was accurately interpreted by Daniel, I noted that we would discuss the dream's prophetic content here in chapter 8. I did so for three reasons. First, I wanted to focus on the background and story of Daniel before we focused on the prophecies in the text. Second, because the prophetic dream was given to Nebuchadnezzar, not Daniel. Third, and most importantly, the statue prophecy in Daniel chapter 2 parallels the prophecy Daniel recorded in chapter 7. Viewing them together is extremely compelling and eye-opening.

Statues

First, let's take a quick look at the statue dream in Daniel chapter 2. In the interpretation, we read:

> After you, another kingdom will arise, inferior to yours. Next, a third kingdom, one of bronze, will rule over the whole earth. Finally, there will be a fourth kingdom, strong as iron—for iron breaks and smashes everything—and as iron breaks things to pieces, so it will crush and break all the others. Just as you saw that the feet and toes were partly of baked clay and partly of iron, so this will be a divided kingdom; yet it will have some of the strength of iron in it, even as you saw iron mixed with clay. As the toes were partly iron and partly clay, so this kingdom will be partly strong and partly brittle. And just as you saw the iron mixed with baked clay, so the people will be a mixture and will not remain united, any more than iron mixes with clay (Daniel 2:39-43).

In the Bible, kings and kingdoms are synonymous. Notice right from the outset of what we just read that Nebuchadnezzar himself is seen as a kingdom, as indicated by the phrase "after you, another kingdom will arise." This is common throughout Scripture. So, in this sweeping prophecy we see that Babylon will be followed by three successive empires, each one taking over from the previous empire. Each empire is represented by types of metal as the prophecy moves down the statue from head to toes. Toward the end of the fourth kingdom the materials become an unstable mix of metal and clay in the feet and the toes. During the time of the ten toes, a divine rock will strike the toes and turn the statue to dust, thus ending the succession of Gentile kingdoms, then the rock becomes an all-encompassing mountain (Daniel 2:44-45).

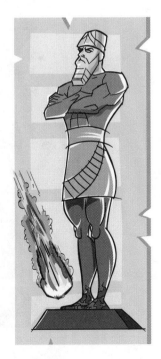

Woah! There is a lot to unpack here. God masterfully compresses a maximum amount of information into a minimum number of words. There is more information provided in the analysis of the prophecy than in the prophecy itself. In a feeling similar to knowing a good movie by still thinking about its meaning days after you first watched it, prophecy enriches you when its details unveil more and more information the longer you contemplate its meaning.

Observation is the most overlooked component to interpretation. When I was a student in seminary, one of my courses on hermeneutics (Bible interpretation) gave me a lesson in this very area. The class was given the assignment to come up with 25 observations from a single verse. The verse was Acts 1:8. We were instructed to provide no interpretation or mention of any other portions of Scripture, strictly to produce observations directly from that one verse. It was tough. But not as tough as our next assignment, which was to use the same verse and make 25 new observations. Finally, we had a third assignment. You guessed it, make 25 more unique observations using the same verse. All told, we came up with over 75 observations from one single verse! When we slow down long enough to observe the text's details, we find a treasure trove of particulars that help us to understand what the Bible is saying.

As we observe the details of the vision of the statue and compare it with history that has occurred since then we see something incredible. The prophecy accurately predicted that the Babylonian Empire—the head of gold—would be conquered by the Medo-Persian Empire, represented by the silver torso with two arms. The Medo-Persians would be conquered by the Greek Empire—the belly and thighs of bronze. The Greeks would be conquered by the Roman Empire—legs of iron—which split in two (east and west). The Roman Empire would then collapse from within and break apart into various nation-states— some weak, some strong. This is exactly what has happened. It appears that the only parts of the prophecy that are yet to take place are represented by the feet and toes of the statue and the divine rock that turns into a mountain. We'll discuss those in Section 3 of this book, where we study the yet-future fulfillments and end-times aspects of Daniel's prophecies.

Consider these additional details about the statue and how they further support the incredible fulfillment of this sweeping prophecy. The materials decrease in value as you move down the statue. At the same time, the materials increase in strength from the top to the bottom—until you get to the feet, which are unstable. This lines up with history as well. The successive empires became less and less wealthy, and more and more focused on conquest. They were each characterized by the very metals that were represented in the statue.

Here are some additional compelling observations to note. Nebuchadnezzar was designated as the head of the statue and representative of all the Gentile empires (even though the Egyptian and Syrian empires came before his). This is fitting because the very idea of world empires originated in Babylon, when you recall the Tower of Babel rebellion from Genesis 11. Also, the head of the statue had absolute authority. Literally, Nebuchadnezzar's word was law.

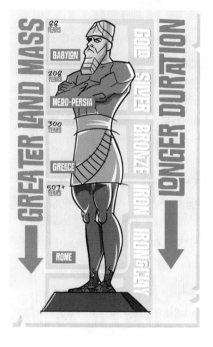

GREATER LAND MASS

88 YEARS — BABYLON

208 YEARS — MEDO-PERSIA

300 YEARS — GREECE

507+ YEARS — ROME

GOLD SILVER BRONZE IRON IRON/CLAY

LONGER DURATION

He was an absolute monarch. And, the succession of leaders who followed him had increasingly less authority—sharing power with the rule of law, other co-rulers, or representatives of the people.

We also discover that each of these empires encompassed greater land mass and lasted longer than the one that preceded it. The Babylonian Empire lasted 88 years, the Medo-Persian Empire lasted 208 years, the empire of Greece lasted 300 years, and the Roman Empire lasted 507 years in its most complete form—1,484 years when you include how long the eastern leg of the empire ruled.

The successive kingdoms of Babylon, Medo-Persia, Greece, and Rome, followed by the Roman Empire splitting into two legs (fulfilled in AD 395 when the Eastern leg separated from Rome and established its capital in Constantinople, which is modern-day Istanbul), then breaking into individual nation-states, is an accurate description of history. And notice that no empire has ever conquered the Roman Empire. It collapsed from within, then broke up into nation-states, many of which maintain the Roman style of law and government. Various world leaders such as Charlemagne, Napoleon, Hitler, and Mussolini have attempted to bring about a new European empire. All of man's efforts toward this goal have failed because the end of the fourth empire—fragmented pieces of iron and clay that don't mix well—is the final Gentile kingdom in the prophecy before the future millennial kingdom of Christ.

QUICK FACT: DID YOU KNOW...

that the first century Jewish historian Josephus understood the Daniel 2 statue prophecy as representing Babylon, Medo-Persia, Greece, Rome, and a final future kingdom?[12]

Prophecy experts differ in opinion on what part of the statue represents yet-future prophecy today. They vary slightly on the nature of the transition from the Roman Empire represented by the iron legs and the feet of mixed clay and iron. Some cite a gap between the legs and the feet, with the feet and toes being strictly end-times configurations. Other experts understand the sections of the statue as continuous from Daniel's time right up until the time of the end. I tend to agree with the latter, although I am not dogmatic. We'll tackle this in more depth in chapter 11, where we'll study the yet-future aspects of this prophecy. Now let's compare the statue from Daniel chapter 2 with the beasts in Daniel chapter 7.

Beasts

Daniel chapter 7 is the first of four extremely detailed visions that were given directly to the prophet Daniel. Chapter 7 lies on the hinge of the book of Daniel, dividing the narrative and prophetic sections of the book.

In Daniel chapter 2, we get a glimpse of world empires as seen from a human vantage point. The statue depicts a man, made up of shiny metals. In Daniel chapter 7, we get to view the same prophetic succession of empires; however, we see them from a different vantage point. We see them for what they really are—horrifying beasts.

Even today, humans have a lofty vision of themselves when they disregard the fact of original sin—the biblical teaching that we are all born with a sin nature. We are not sinners just because we sin. We sin because we are

THE KINGDOMS

GOLD
SILVER
BRONZE
IRON
IRON/CLAY

BABYLON
612 BC

MEDO-PERSIA
539 BC

GREECE
330 BC

ROME
63 BC

REVIVED ROME
END-TIMES
CONFIGURATION

DANIEL 2   DANIEL 7

sinners. It is in our nature. Well, in Daniel 7, we see God's point of view to recognize what sinful world empires are really made of.

If God says something once, we should take note. When God gives us two extremely detailed prophecies about the same topic, we should really pay attention! With the details of Daniel 2 fresh in your mind, let's read this from Daniel 7:3-7:

> Four great beasts, each different from the others, came up out of the sea. The first was like a lion, and it had the wings of an eagle. I watched until its wings were torn off and it was lifted from the ground so that it stood on two feet like a human being, and the mind of a human was given to it.

> And there before me was a second beast, which looked like a bear. It was raised up on one of its sides, and it had three ribs in its mouth between its teeth. It was told, "Get up and eat your fill of flesh!"

After that, I looked, and there before me was another beast, one that looked like a leopard. And on its back it had four wings like those of a bird. This beast had four heads, and it was given authority to rule.

After that, in my vision at night I looked, and there before me was a fourth beast—terrifying and frightening and very powerful. It had large iron teeth; it crushed and devoured its victims and trampled underfoot whatever was left. It was different from all the former beasts, and it had ten horns.

Following this description, Daniel graciously included the interpretation for us (given directly to him by an angelic being). We read this in Daniel 7:17-18:

The four great beasts are four kings that will rise from the earth. But the holy people of the Most High will receive the kingdom and will possess it forever—yes, for ever and ever.

So, right there we are given the synopsis of the prophecy—a prophecy that parallels the prophecy from Daniel chapter 2, interpreted by Daniel roughly 50 years earlier when Nebuchadnezzar was king.

These descriptions of the beasts also line up with what we know about the history of the four empires. Babylon is seen as a lion. It was first of the empires in the prophecy—king of the beasts, so to speak. And the eagle is king of the birds of prey. Reliefs of winged lions were often used on the doors of Babylonian palaces. In Scripture, Babylon is associated with the lion and the eagle (Jeremiah 4:7, 13; Ezekiel 17:3). In the prophecy, the wings of the lion get clipped and it stands on its feet like a man. This could reference Nebuchadnezzar's humbling after living like an animal, or it could also point to the decline of his empire after his death.

Next, we read the description of a bear—second in line after the lion (see 1 Samuel 17:34). The bear was stronger on one side than the other. Historically, the Persian side of the Medo-Persian Empire was notably more prominent. The three ribs present in the bear's mouth have been interpreted a few different ways. The most compelling that I've come across is that the Medo-Persian Empire encompassed all three areas of Media, Persia, and Babylon.

The third beast in the prophecy is depicted as a leopard with four wings and four heads. Like the leopard, Greece's armies were known for their speed and agility. Alexander the Great is named as such because of his leadership of a military that was able to conquer with swiftness and efficiency unmatched by any before him. The four wings on the back of the leopard also speak to its speed. In football and basketball terms, Greece was known for its hurry-up offense and its full-court press.

Alexander the Great lived fast and died young. He was 20 years old when he began expanding his empire and spreading Hellenistic influence. By the age of 26, he had conquered the entire Medo-Persian Empire. By almost 33, he was dead (possibly poisoned), and his realm was left without an heir. Eventually, the empire—that had four governmental divisions—was divided into four parts under the leadership of four of Alexander the Great's generals. It took roughly 20 years, but the empire was ultimately divided into Greece, western Asia, Egypt, and Persia.

ALEXANDER THE GREAT

Finally in the prophecy, a fourth beast replaced the previous empire and was known for its brutality and iron teeth. If you have studied anything about the Roman Empire, you'll note that this is an apt description. A last detail about this beast—interestingly enough, found at the very end of the prophecy—is the mention of its ten horns. Like the ten toes of the Daniel 2 prophecy, we'll save our discussion about this characteristic for chapter 11.

Today, I find it very interesting that the nations of the world often use various animals or beasts to symbolize themselves. The United States and the bald eagle. England and the lion. Russia and the bear. China and the dragon. Dominant world nations seem to intuitively identify with this Gentile nation beast theme found in Daniel chapter 7.

The Kingdom Context Continues

As we continue to see, Daniel is a book of kingdoms. Specifically, showing the contrast between the kingdoms of man and the kingdom of God. Both prophecies in Daniel 2 and Daniel 7 tell of a fifth and final kingdom. We will also discuss this kingdom in chapter 11 of this book. In the meantime, our present takeaway is recognizing that God's sovereign hand is guiding history just as predicted in Daniel chapters 2 and 7. These 2,600-year-old prophecies outlining the succession of world empires and the time of the end are so grand in scope and accurate in their description that Bible critics either have to ignore them or invent weak arguments in an attempt to explain away their accuracy.

The prophecies found in Daniel chapters 2 and 7 contain the broadest sweep of world history that the Lord ever gave to any of the Old Testament prophets! Ponder again the fact that the fulfillments of these prophecies span from 605 BC through world history to the future millennial kingdom, and into the eternal state. Consider that from an apologetics standpoint for a moment. These epic examples of comprehensive historical prophecy—perfectly fulfilled thus far—serves as concrete evidence the Bible is supernatural in nature. Only God can predict the future with such incredible clarity, boldness, and accuracy.

From these prophecies we can conclude that God is completely sovereign over the schemes and plans of godless rulers that will ultimately come to nothing. The facts of history bear witness to the predicted decline of nations. We should expect the nations to become increasingly unstable in the last days. All the indicating factors of disunity inform us we are nearing the time when Jesus will return to destroy his enemies and set everything straight. These are indeed very exciting times!

CHAPTER 9

The G.O.A.T. Beats the Ram

Remember the former things, those of long ago; I am God, and there is no other; I am God, and there is none like me. I make known the end from the beginning, from ancient times, what is still to come. I say, "My purpose will stand, and I will do all that I please."

ISAIAH 46:9-10

In the world of sports, commentators and fans often debate who is the G.O.A.T. in various athletic disciplines. The acronym stands for "greatest of all time." In basketball, Michael Jordan is often cited. For football, Tom Brady. In boxing, Sugar Ray Robinson. Obviously, these designations are difficult to quantify, and the topic is regularly debated with many prominent names placed into the conversations. However, when it comes to the very different subject of ancient military history, nearly all historians agree that Alexander the Great was truly the G.O.A.T. People are surprised to learn that his military exploits (and many other details) were recorded before they happened, through

LISTEN, YOU MAY THINK YOU ARE THE G.O.A.T., BUT I'M THE G.O.A.T.

a vision that God gave to Daniel, 200 years before Alexander appeared on the world stage. Daniel chapter 8 records Daniel's description of this vision, as well as the angel Gabriel's interpretation of it.

Speaking of G.O.A.T.s—the Bible is the greatest book of all time, and the book of Daniel helps prove it. The Bible is the only written record that: (1) claims to be the very word of God and (2) backs up this claim through fulfilled prophecy. The verses at the opening of this chapter make a bold claim and provide immediate feedback to either verify or debunk the claims of Scripture.

The prophecies of Daniel are either supernatural and reliable, or they are a complete fabrication. If Daniel did not record the words of his book under the inspiration of the Holy Spirit (2 Peter 1:21) before the events occurred, then what we read in the book of Daniel is fraudulent and cannot be taken seriously. However, if it can be demonstrated that the book of Daniel was written in advance of the prophesied events detailed therein, then it is obvious that the prophecies recorded for us are not merely human words.

The primary reason for mentioning this now is because the prophecies recorded in Daniel 8 (as well as those we will study in Daniel 11) are so incredibly detailed in their descriptions and accurate in their fulfillments, that critics have argued that the book was not written by the prophet or during the time period described therein. They claim that the book of Daniel must have been written (or amended) after the events described in his prophecies had occurred.

Prior to 1947, these critics would often cite that the oldest manuscript copy of the book of Daniel known to exist was from AD 900—some 1,400 years after the book was written, and more than 1,200 years after the events prophesied in Daniel chapter 8. The manuscript from AD 900 was a copy of the Septuagint (the Greek translation of the Old Testament, from 285 BC). The critics claimed that Daniel's detailed prophecies must have been added (all at once or in phases) to the book of Daniel sometime during the first century AD and following.

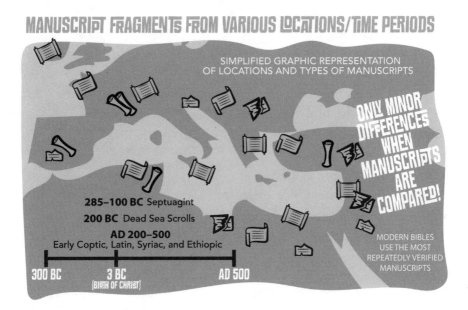

MANUSCRIPT FRAGMENTS FROM VARIOUS LOCATIONS/TIME PERIODS

SIMPLIFIED GRAPHIC REPRESENTATION
OF LOCATIONS AND TYPES OF MANUSCRIPTS

ONLY MINOR DIFFERENCES WHEN MANUSCRIPTS ARE COMPARED!

285–100 BC Septuagint
200 BC Dead Sea Scrolls
AD 200–500
Early Coptic, Latin, Syriac, and Ethiopic

300 BC   3 BC
            (BIRTH OF CHRIST)   AD 500

MODERN BIBLES
USE THE MOST
REPEATEDLY VERIFIED
MANUSCRIPTS

However, when the Dead Sea Scrolls were discovered in 1947 and in the years following, they demonstrated that the book of Daniel had already been used and copied by the people at Qumran prior to 200 BC. Manuscript fragments that included nearly all the book of Daniel proved that the content of Daniel had not changed at all. This game-changing discovery shows once again that God's Word has been reliably preserved through the ages, and that many of the prophecies it contains have come to pass exactly as foretold.

Previously, because the oldest manuscript copy known to exist was from AD 900, critics asserted that the incredibly accurate details of the prophecies in the book of Daniel were added after the fact in order to sensationalize the text. But the discovery of the Dead Sea Scrolls blew their assertions out of the water. Many of the now accurately fulfilled prophecies had not yet occurred by 200 BC, and the content of the book of Daniel was shown not to have changed at all between 200 BC and AD 900! As with the Babylonian Chronicles we looked at in chapter 6 of this book, the critics' assertions were once again proven incorrect.

The only explanation for the accuracy of the fulfilled prophecies in the book of Daniel is that the book (along with every other book in the canon of Scripture) is divinely inspired. Over and over, the historical record of the Bible proves to be true, and the prophecies contained in Scripture come to pass exactly as foretold. Few places in Scripture have the level of prophetic detail  as Daniel chapters 8 and 11. Now, with the reliability of the book firmly established, let's look at the breathtaking chapter 8, which describes another one of Daniel's visions.

Two Languages for Two Programs

Daniel chapter 8 marks another pivotal change in the book. While Daniel is split into two sections of historical narrative (chapters 1–6) and predictive prophecy (chapters 7–12), it is also written in two languages determined by what audience it was primarily intended for, either Gentile or Jewish.

Daniel 1–2:4a was written in Hebrew, and Daniel 2:4b through the end of chapter 7 is in Aramaic. In chapter 8, Daniel returns to using the Hebrew language with a very specific and intentional focus on God's prophetic plans for the Jewish people and the land of Israel. This remains the case all the way through Daniel chapter 12. A careful study of the book of Daniel—and the Bible as a whole—makes it abundantly clear that God has two distinct programs: one for the Jewish people, and one for the rest of humanity. In other words, the church has not replaced Israel.

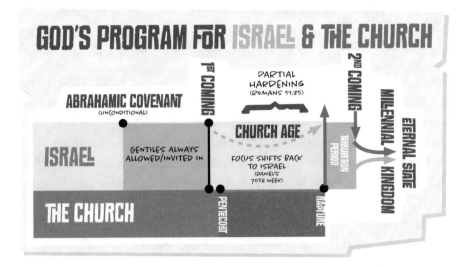

GOD'S PROGRAM FOR ISRAEL & THE CHURCH

1ST COMING

PARTIAL HARDENING
(ROMANS 11:25)

2ND COMING

MILLENNIAL KINGDOM

ETERNAL STATE

ABRAHAMIC COVENANT
(UNCONDITIONAL)

CHURCH AGE

TRIBULATION PERIOD

ISRAEL

GENTILES ALWAYS
ALLOWED/INVITED IN

FOCUS SHIFTS BACK
TO ISRAEL
(DANIEL'S
70TH WEEK)

THE CHURCH

PENTECOST

RAPTURE

The church has been—as Paul so eloquently puts it in Romans 12—grafted into God's plan of salvation. All individuals must accept Christ and his work on the cross to obtain salvation, but in terms of God's prophetic plans for the ages and the future fulfillment of specific prophecies related to Israel and the Jewish people, God has two distinct but related plans for Israel and the church—both of which beautifully culminate in the end. I've written extensively on this in my other books, so I won't labor the point here except to draw attention to how this dual program is evident even in the structure of Daniel's book. This is extremely important to understand as we study the prophecies found in Daniel chapters 8–12—particularly Daniel chapter 9, which contains the single most important prophecy found in the book of Daniel. But you'll have to wait until chapter 13 before we unpack that prophecy.

Daniel's Second Vision

Daniel opens chapter 8 with a specific time cue. He states that he received the vision in the third year of King Belshazzar's reign. He also mentions that this vision came after the prophetic vision he recorded in chapter 7 regarding the four beasts. So, this vision described in Daniel 8 would have been given in 551 BC, before the incident of the handwriting on the wall, and it is the second vision that was given directly to Daniel. In Daniel chapters 2 and 5, the prophet interpreted God's messages to others, but in chapters 7 and 8, Daniel describes prophetic visions given directly to him. Daniel would have been roughly 70 years of age when he received this prophetic vision.

Another interesting detail to note is that in verse 2 of chapter 8, Daniel points out that he saw himself in Susa, the capital of Persia in the province of Elam (in modern-day southern Iran, just north of the Persian Gulf). Daniel's vision indicated he would outlive the Babylonian Empire and find himself in the heart of the Persian empire. It seems Daniel was spiritually transported to Susa. There are other examples in Scripture of believers being transported. Ezekiel was transported to Jerusalem (Ezekiel 8:3). John was transported to a wilderness (Revelation 17:3). And the apostle Paul was transported to heaven, but wasn't sure whether he was in the spirit or in the body (2 Corinthians 12:2-3).

QUICK FACT: DID YOU KNOW...

that Nehemiah (Nehemiah 1:1) and Esther (Esther 1:2-5; 2:5-7) would both live in Susa?

From Susa, the prophet describes the vision of a ram with two horns (with one horn younger, yet longer than the other), charging to the west, north, and south without anything or anyone able to stop its advance. It became very great. Then suddenly, a single-horned goat came from the west, flying rapidly across the earth, shattering the two horns of the ram and defeating it. Next, Daniel describes the great goat having its horn broken off at the height of its power. Four new prominent horns grew in its place (Daniel 8:3-8).

This prophecy was given 200 years prior to its fulfillment. All credible experts (and the critics who dispute the dating of Daniel's writings as coming after the fact) agree that the ram represents Alexander the Great. The details of the prophecy relate to specific historical aspects of his military campaigns and the division of his empire after his untimely death. The context of Scripture makes it clear that horns are associated with power and rulership. God's vision to Daniel contains a common symbol present in the Bible—horns—to identify the rulers of empires and geographic areas.

Four Prominent Horns

Alexander the Great and his comparatively small army conquered the entire Medo-Persian Empire (and then some) in just under three years. Alexander was a tactical genius and almost effortlessly defeated armies with much larger numbers. He did so in notoriously swift fashion. Alexander the Great died when he was not quite 33 years old, and his empire was split into four realms that were eventually ruled by four of his generals. The "four prominent horns" of Daniel 8:8 are those generals, of whom are also depicted by the four heads of the leopard beast we saw in the last chapter, from Daniel 7:6.

QUICK FACT: DID YOU KNOW...

the historian Josephus recorded that Alexander the Great was shown Daniel chapter 8 by the high priest, Jaddua, and realized that he (Alexander) was the goat in the prophecy? This incident impacted Alexander so much that he spared Jerusalem.[13]

These generals are important to know because they appear in prophecies in Daniel chapters 8 and 11 and they impacted key historical developments during the intertestamental period—the period between the completion of the Old Testament and the events described in the record of the New Testament. These are the four generals and the approximate geographic areas they oversaw within 20 years of the death of Alexander the Great:

- Ptolemy: Egypt and Israel
- Seleucus: Syria, Mesopotamia, and eastward
- Lysimachus: Asia Minor
- Antipater or his son, Cassander (experts differ on which one): Macedonia and Greece

Another Horn

In an earlier chapter, I mentioned the mountain peaks of Bible prophecy. Often, prophets would record prophecies with details that had both near-future and distant-future aspects to them. For example, many messianic prophecies from the Old Testament describe aspects of both the first coming of Christ and his second coming in the same passage; sometimes even in the same sentence. Similar to how a person can view multiple mountain peaks simultaneously even though those peaks may be separated by great distances, prophets would provide details about future events side-by-side, even though they will later prove to be separated by hundreds or even thousands of years.

THE MOUNTAIN PEAKS OF BIBLE PROPHECY

FRONT VIEW   **SIDE VIEW**

I mention that here because, in the next part of Daniel's vision, the prophet jumps forward another 200 years to prophecies about a historical figure we now know as Antiochus Epiphanes. Beginning in Daniel 8:9, we read about "another horn" that would arise out of the four-part division of the Greek Empire. Daniel 8:9-12 reads:

> Out of one of them came another horn, which started small but grew in power to the south and to the east and toward the Beautiful Land. It grew until it reached the host of the heavens, and it threw some of the starry host down to the earth and trampled on them. It set itself up to be as great as the commander of the army of the LORD; it took away the daily sacrifice from the LORD, and his sanctuary was thrown down. Because of rebellion, the LORD's people and the daily sacrifice were given over to it. It prospered in everything it did, and truth was thrown to the ground.

As recorded in history, the eighth king of the Seleucid dynasty, Antiochus IV Epiphanes, did exactly as was foretold. Antiochus Epiphanes ruled Syria from 175 to 164 BC. The records of 1 and 2 Maccabees and those of the Jewish historian Josephus detail the events of this period and record the persecution of the Jewish people by this notable historical figure.

ANTIOCHUS IV

Antiochus made efforts to expand the Seleucid Empire and nearly took Egypt but failed. He then turned his focus to his infamous, intense persecution of the Jewish people. After ongoing conflict between the Hellenists and the Traditionalists (two Jewish factions at the time), Antiochus outlawed the system of Jewish law and worship. He commanded the worship of Zeus and attempted to remove all key facets of Jewish culture and religious practice.

This conflict reached a tipping point in 167 BC, when Antiochus had his forces raid the temple in Jerusalem, loot it, and set up an altar to worship Zeus. To bring even more offense to the Jewish people, pigs—unclean animals according to Mosaic law—were sacrificed on the temple altar. This act became known as the "abomination of desolation" (see Daniel 8:13).

Antiochus pushed the Jewish people to their limit, and when they rebelled, he killed a large number of them and sold many into slavery. He doubled down on his oppressive measures by making circumcision punishable by death, commanding Jewish people to make sacrifices to pagan gods, and ordering them to eat pig meat.

This ongoing brutal oppression led to what is known as the Maccabean revolt, a Jewish resistance movement led by Judas Maccabeus and his family, who organized several victorious attacks against the forces of Antiochus Epiphanes. After recapturing the temple, the Maccabees cleansed and restored it to use in 164 BC.

The Jewish holiday known as Hanukkah celebrates this victory and the restoration of the temple. People are often surprised to learn that a reference to Hanukkah is found in the New Testament. The holiday is referred to in the book of John as the Festival of Dedication (see John 10:22-23).

Antiochus Epiphanes serves as a prototype of an evil end-times figure. During the future tribulation period the antichrist will follow in the footsteps of Antiochus, but in a significantly broader and more horrific way. We'll take a closer look at the yet-future aspects of this prophecy in section 3 of this book.

A Little Help from Above

For the interpretation of the vision, the Lord sent the archangel Gabriel which caused Daniel to fall into a deep sleep. This is the first mention in Scripture of the specific name of one of God's good angels. Gabriel shows up again in Daniel 9:21 and Luke 1:19, 26, each time delivering prophecies related to the Jewish people. Also in the book of Daniel, the angel Michael appears in Daniel 10:13, 21 and 12:1; he is mentioned later in the Bible in Jude 9 and Revelation 12:7. For a deeper study on all things related to angels and spiritual warfare, you may want to read my book, *The Non-Prophet's Guide*™ *to Spiritual Warfare.*

In Daniel 8:19-22, the archangel Gabriel shared this with Daniel:

> I am going to tell you what will happen later in the time of wrath, because the vision concerns the appointed time of the end. The two-horned ram that you saw represents the kings of Media and Persia. The shaggy goat is the king of Greece, and the large horn between its eyes is the first king. The four horns that replaced the one that was broken off represent four kingdoms that will emerge from his nation but will not have the same power.

The beauty of prophecy and prophetic symbolism in Scripture is that we don't have to guess at the meanings. The meanings of the prophecies and symbols are often given in the immediate context (as seen here), or in the broader context of Scripture. In Revelation, for example, roughly half of the symbols used are interpreted for us in the text, and the remaining are understood by looking at the broader context of Scripture—particularly (but not exclusively) here in the book of Daniel. If you want to understand Revelation, then study the book of Daniel. The Bible has one Ultimate Author, therefore the symbolism is all in harmony, even though the Bible was written over a period of roughly 1,500 years by at least 40 different individuals.

66 BOOKS
40+ WRITERS
3 CONTINENTS
1500 YEARS
1 STORY
39 OT | 27 NT

Sealed to Unsealed

Gabriel's final admonition to Daniel was to "seal up the vision" because it has to do with the "distant future" (Daniel 8:26). Interestingly, when John wrote the book of Revelation, he was told not to "seal up the words of the prophecy" (Revelation 22:10). With the completion of the canon of Scripture, emphasized by the capstone of prophecy and the crescendo of God's story, prophecy became unsealed. The full picture had been painted for us, ready to study and contemplate as we await the Lord's return in the church age.

Daniel was sealed but Revelation was left unsealed. We have the full revelation of God's Word and we know the broad brushstrokes of how everything will play out. What a blessing! However, we do not know the exact timing of future events or all of the details about them, so we must be like Daniel, and follow his lead from the final verse of the chapter. It reads, "I, Daniel, was worn out. I lay exhausted for several days. Then I got up and went about the king's business. I was appalled by the vision; it was beyond understanding" (Daniel 8:27).

There is a lesson here. When we interact with Bible prophecy, we may become weary and we will struggle to understand all things prophetic. With the complete picture given to us through the unsealed book of Revelation, with the complete biblical canon available for us to study, and with stage-setting events for the future tribulation taking place today, we have been given some astounding clarity. However, there are mysteries that remain, and that is okay. Let us get up and go about the King's business! We need to remain dedicated to serving in the world around us. Let us focus our time, energy, and resources on reaching others for Christ and living godly lives as we do so.

CHAPTER 10

Delayed Delivery of a Divine Directive

Do not be afraid, Daniel. Since the first day that you set your mind to gain understanding and to humble yourself before your God, your words were heard, and I have come in response to them.

DANIEL 10:12

DANIEL

We are here.

1 2 3 4 5 6 7 8 9 10 11 12

HISTORICAL NARRATIVE   PREDICTIVE PROPHECY

In the third year of Cyrus, roughly 72 years after Daniel was taken to Babylon as a teenager, the prophet was likely in his eighties when he received another vision.

By this time, Cyrus had issued the decree that allowed the Jews to return to their land. Also, two years prior, Daniel had finished his career of service in the king's court (Daniel 1:21). It appears that even though Daniel had been praying for his people to return to their land after the 70 years of captivity were fulfilled (see Jeremiah 29:10; Daniel 9:1-2), the prophet himself remained in exile. Perhaps Daniel felt the trip back home would be too taxing on him, or that he would better serve his people by remaining where he was. In any

case, Daniel was quite old by the time he received this fourth and final vision from the Lord.

You may be thinking to yourself, *Wait a minute—we are missing a third vision here and we haven't looked at Daniel chapter 9.* We'll discuss Daniel 9 and his third vision later in chapter 13 of this book. Here in section 2, we are looking at already-fulfilled prophecies, of which there are many in Daniel 10 and 11.

In these two chapters of Daniel, the prophet describes the event of his fourth and final vision. Daniel 10 provides the context of the vision, and in chapter 11, Daniel recorded the vision itself. Chapter 10 gives us great insight into the relationship between spiritual warfare, prayer, and prophecy. And chapter 11 provides us with one of the most detailed prophecies in the entire Bible. Daniel 11:1-35 accurately foretells many specific details of key intertestamental historical facts. The fulfillment of these details was so accurate that critics have often attacked the dating of Daniel's writings. But as highlighted in previous chapters, archeology continues to prove that Daniel was written prior to the events prophesied.

The Introduction to the Vision

Chapter 10 serves as a long windup to Daniel's fourth and final vision. Then chapter 11 contains the vision (which extends into chapter 12 as well, but we'll cover the yet-future prophecies of chapter 12 in another chapter). So, the final 3 chapters of Daniel serve as the crescendo of the book, much like the book of Revelation serves as the grand finale for the canon of Scripture.

Within the introduction to the vision in chapter 10 we find many interesting details, such as Daniel's practice of prayer and fasting when seeking God's intervention, mind-blowing insight about angelic beings and how they operate, the practice of spiritual warfare and how fallen angels oversee geographic territories and specific responsibilities in the unseen realm, and the consistent language surrounding God's unified—yet distinct—plans for the people of Israel and for the Gentiles.

The occasion of the vision came as a result of Daniel's fasting and praying. This would have been after his people had been allowed—by decree of King Cyrus as prophesied in Isaiah 44 and 45—to return to their homeland. Daniel likely heard about the struggles to rebuild as reports came in about Ezra and Nehemiah, who faced challenges there.

QUICK FACT: DID YOU KNOW...

that the prophet Isaiah predicted a king named Cyrus from Persia would give a command to return to Jerusalem to rebuild the city and the temple 150 years before he (Cyrus) lived and before Israel was taken captive?
(Read about it in Isaiah 44:28; 45:1,4.)

Because of Daniel's dedication, he was visited by an angel (or possibly a few different angels). The people who were with Daniel could not see what Daniel saw (10:7), and once again, Daniel fell into a deep sleep. It's important to note that every time a person in Scripture sees an angel in their full glory, they are terrified. Angels can disguise themselves as men (Genesis 19:1-3, 15-16; Hebrews 13:2), but whenever they show themselves in their natural glorified form, those who see them are terrified and need to be revived or encouraged not to be afraid.

Here, we get a glimpse of how spiritual warfare works as well. In Daniel 10:12-14, we read:

> Do not be afraid, Daniel. Since the first day that you set your mind
> to gain understanding and to humble yourself before your God,

your words were heard, and I have come in response to them. But the prince of the Persian kingdom resisted me twenty-one days. Then Michael, one of the chief princes, came to help me, because I was detained there with the king of Persia. Now I have come to explain to you what will happen to your people in the future, for the vision concerns a time yet to come.

As is often the case, particularly here in the book of Daniel, when God's people humble themselves and pray, it moves the heart and hand of God. We also find here that delayed answers from God can be the result of spiritual warfare in the unseen realm. Furthermore, we discover that the geographic area of Persia has a fallen angel associated with it.

I discuss this in depth (along with a full systematic study of that topic) in *The Non-Prophet's Guide™ to Spiritual Warfare*. But for the purposes of this book, I'll just draw your attention to the fact that there is an entire network of fallen angels who resist the work of God in both the seen and the unseen realms. Using modern vernacular, there is a parallel universe that we can't see

with our natural eyes, but it is just as real as our physical world, and what happens there impacts the affairs of humans on a daily basis all over the world.

Apparently, the enemy did not want this message delivered because of its vital importance. God was sending advance intel to Daniel about what would happen to the Jewish people in the future. Satan hates the Jewish people. Make no mistake about it, spiritual warfare is at the root of antisemitism. Satan hates them because they are God's chosen people through whom the Messiah came and it is their corporate salvation (Romans 11:26) that will usher in the return of Christ at the end of the tribulation period (Zechariah 12:10; Matthew 23:39; Revelation 12:6, 13-17) to set up the millennial kingdom (Revelation 20:1-6), where our Jewish Savior will literally rule and reign from Jerusalem (2 Samuel 7:12-13).

The Vision

Now for the incredibly detailed prophetic vision that is described in Daniel chapters 11 and 12. As mentioned above, I'll cover the fulfilled prophecies of chapter 11 here, and the yet-future prophecies in an upcoming chapter. My reason for dividing the book this way is to focus on the apologetic nature of the fulfilled prophecies before turning our attention to the truly amazing yet-future prophecies.

Keep in mind, the specific framework for the prophetic details we're about to discover is that they relate to Daniel's people. In biblical prophetic terms, the focal point of prophecy is Jerusalem and the Jewish people. With that established, Daniel was given prophecies related to the near future (from his perspective). In Daniel 11:2-34, there are no fewer than 30 specific prophetic details, all of which came to pass exactly as foretold. Here is a concise overview of these details from this short passage.

30 KEY PROPHECIES: Daniel 11:2-34

THE YEAR THE PROPHECIES WERE GIVEN: Third year of King Cyrus (10:1)—537 BC

HISTORICAL FULFILLMENT PERIOD: 529–164 BC[14]

> ### Prophecy #1
>
> **11:2a**—"Three more kings will arise in Persia"
>
> *Historical Fulfillment:* Cambyses, Pseudo-Smerdis, and Darius I
>
> ### Prophecy #2
>
> **11:2b**—"…and then a fourth, who will be far richer than all the others. When he has gained power by his wealth, he will stir up everyone against the kingdom of Greece."
>
> *Historical Fulfillment:* Xerxes I

Prophecy #3

11:3—"Then a mighty king will arise, who will rule with great power and do as he pleases."

Historical Fulfillment: Alexander the Great

ALEXANDER THE GREAT

Prophecy #4

11:4—"After he has arisen, his empire will be broken up and parceled out toward the four winds of heaven. It will not go to his descendants, nor will it have the power he exercised, because his empire will be uprooted and given to others."

Historical Fulfillment: Macedon and Greece were given to Cassander; Thrace and Asia Minor were given to Lysimachus; Suria and Babylon were given to Seleucus; Judah and Egypt were given to Ptolemy.

Prophecy #5

11:5a—"The king of the South will become strong"

Historical Fulfillment: Ptolemy I Soter

Prophecy #6

11:5b—"but one of his commanders will become even stronger than he and will rule his own kingdom with great power."

Historical Fulfillment: Seleucus I Nicator took over Babylon and other areas.

Prophecy #7

11:6a—"After some years, they will become allies. The daughter of the king of the South will go to the king of the North to make an alliance,"

Historical Fulfillment: Ptolemy II Philadelphus sent his daughter Berenice to marry Antiochus II Theos to form an alliance.

Prophecy #8

11:6b—"but she will not retain her power, and he and his power will not last. In those days she will be betrayed, together with her royal escort and her father and the one who supported her."

Historical Fulfillment: Antiochus II's first wife, Laodice, conspired to have he and Berenice killed. Ptolemy II died around the same time.

Prophecy #9

11:7-8a—"One from her family line will arise to take her place. He will attack the forces of the king of the North and enter his fortress; he will fight against them and be victorious. He will also seize their gods, their metal images and their valuable articles of silver and gold and carry them off to Egypt."

Historical Fulfillment: Berenice's brother, Ptolemy III Euergetes, defeated Seleucus II Callinicus, looted the captured land, and returned to Egypt.

Prophecy #10

11:8b—"For some years he will leave the king of the North alone."

Historical Fulfillment: From 241–223 BC, the two empires had peace with each other.

Prophecy #11

11:9—"Then the king of the North will invade the realm of the king of the South but will retreat to his own country."

Historical Fulfillment: Seleucus II hoped to retake territory from Ptolemy III, but failed to do so.

Prophecy #12

11:10—"His sons will prepare for war and assemble a great army, which will sweep on like an irresistible flood and carry the battle as far as his fortress."

Historical Fulfillment: Antiochus III the Great recaptured Phoenician territory from Ptolemy IV Philopater.

Prophecy #13

11:11-12—"Then the king of the South will march out in a rage and fight against the king of the North, who will raise a large army, but it will be defeated. When the army is carried off, the king of the South will be filled with pride and will slaughter many thousands, yet he will not remain triumphant."

Historical Fulfillment: In 217 BC, Ptolemy IV defeated the army of Antiochus III at the battle of Raphia. Antiochus III lost nearly 10,000 soldiers, and roughly 4,000 more were captured.[15]

Prophecy #14

11:13—"For the king of the North will muster another army, larger than the first; and after several years, he will advance with a huge army fully equipped."

Historical Fulfillment: Antiochus III attempted a second invasion of the coastal region of Syria, following the death of Ptolemy IV.

Prophecy #15

11:14—"In those times many will rise against the king of the South. Those who are violent among your own people will rebel in fulfillment of the vision, but without success."

Historical Fulfillment: A number of pro-Seleucid Jewish fighters teamed up with Antiochus III to support his fight against Egypt.

Prophecy #16

11:15—"Then the king of the North will come and build up siege ramps and will capture a fortified city. The forces of the South will be powerless to resist; even their best troops will not have the strength to stand."

Historical Fulfillment: Antiochus III's army defeated the forces of Ptolemy V Epiphanes at Paneas, near Mount Hermon, and took the city of Sidon.

Prophecy #17

11:16—"The invader will do as he pleases; no one will be able to stand against him. He will establish himself in the Beautiful Land and will have the power to destroy it."

Historical Fulfillment: In 198 BC, after the battle at Paneas, Antiochus III controlled the promised land.

Prophecy #18

11:17—"He will determine to come with the might of his entire kingdom and will make an alliance with the king of the South. And he will give him a daughter in marriage in order to overthrow the kingdom, but his plans will not succeed or help him."

Historical Fulfillment: In 193 BC, Antiochus III sent his daughter, Cleopatra I, to wed Ptolemy V to solidify a peace treaty with Egypt.

Prophecy #19

11:18—"Then he will turn his attention to the coastlands and will take many of them, but a commander will put an end to his insolence and will turn his insolence back on him."

Historical Fulfillment: Antiochus III sought greater expansion and came against territories in Asia Minor and Greece, but Roman forces stepped in and defeated him at Thermopylae, and later, at Magnesia, causing Antiochus III to abandon these conquests.

Prophecy #20

11:19—"After this, he will turn back toward the fortresses of his own country but will stumble and fall, to be seen no more."

Historical Fulfillment: One year after the treaty with Rome, Antiochus III was killed in Elam, while attempting to rob the temple of Bel.

Prophecy #21

11:20—"His successor will send out a tax collector to maintain the royal splendor. In a few years, however, he will be destroyed, yet not in anger or in battle."

Historical Fulfillment: Seleucus IV Philopater rose to power after his father, Antiochus III, died. He sent his finance minister, Heliodorus, to Jerusalem to steal the treasures of the temple. Sometime afterward, Heliodorus apparently assassinated Seleucus IV.

Prophecy #22

11:21—"He will be succeeded by a contemptible person who has not been given the honor of royalty. He will invade the kingdom when its people feel secure, and he will seize it through intrigue."

Historical Fulfillment: After the death of Seleucus IV, his brother took the Seleucid throne with the assistance of the king of Pergamum. The newly installed king adopted the name Antiochus IV Epiphanies, which means "glorious."

ANTIOCHUS IV

Prophecy #23

11:22—"Then an overwhelming army will be swept away before him; both it and a prince of the covenant will be destroyed."

Historical Fulfillment: Antiochus IV defeated the armies of Heliodorus and Ptolemy VI Philometor of Egypt. He also removed the Jewish high priest Onias and sold the position to Onias's brother, Jason.

Prophecy #24

11:23—"After coming to an agreement with him, he will act deceitfully, and with only a few people he will rise to power."

Historical Fulfillment: Antiochus IV capitalized on a power struggle in Egypt by siding with Ptolemy VI, which helped him consolidate his power.

Prophecy #25

11:24—"When the richest provinces feel secure, he will invade them and will achieve what neither his fathers nor his forefathers did. He will distribute plunder, loot and wealth among his followers. He will plot the overthrow of fortresses—but only for a time."

Historical Fulfillment: Antiochus IV broke tradition with those who came before him by using his wealth for bribes, strategically gaining favor with key people.

Prophecy #26

11:25-27—"With a large army he will stir up his strength and courage against the king of the South. The king of the South will wage war with a large and very powerful army, but he will not be able to stand because of the plots devised against him. Those who eat from the king's provisions will try to destroy him; his army will be swept away, and many will fall in battle. The two kings, with their hearts bent on evil, will sit at the same table and lie to each other, but to no avail, because an end will still come at the appointed time."

Historical Fulfillment: Antiochus IV's main goal was to take over Egypt. The Ptolemies attempted to defeat Antiochus IV in battle on multiple occasions but were unsuccessful. The two nations attempted to deceive each other.

Prophecy #27

11:28—"The king of the North will return to his own country with great wealth, but his heart will be set against the holy covenant. He will take action against it and then return to his own country."

Historical Fulfillment: Following his victory in Egypt, Antiochus IV stopped in Jerusalem long enough to raid the temple.

Prophecy #28

11:29-30—"At the appointed time he will invade the South again, but this time the outcome will be different from what it was before. Ships of the western coastlands will oppose him, and he will lose heart. Then he will turn back and vent his fury against the holy covenant. He will return and show favor to those who forsake the holy covenant."

Historical Fulfillment: Again Antiochus IV attacked Egypt, but he was forced by the Romans to withdraw. Full of rage, he vented his anger against Jerusalem and the Jewish people on his way back home. He joined forces with Jewish factions who were Hellenized—people who had adopted the Greek way of life—and set out to eliminate the customs of religious Jewish people.

Prophecy #29

11:31—"His armed forces will rise up to desecrate the temple fortress and will abolish the daily sacrifice. Then they will set up the abomination that causes desolation."

Historical Fulfillment: Antiochus IV desecrated the Jewish temple and the altar by converting the temple into an altar of worship to Zeus.

Prophecy #30

11:32-35—"With flattery he will corrupt those who have violated the covenant, but the people who know their God will firmly resist him. Those who are wise will instruct many, though for a time they will fall by the sword or be burned or captured or plundered. When they fall, they will receive a little help, and many who are not sincere will join them. Some of the wise will stumble, so that they may be refined, purified and made spotless until the time of the end, for it will still come at the appointed time."

Historical Fulfillment: Antiochus IV's harsh treatment of the Jewish people led to an uprising led by the Maccabees. Thousands of people were killed during this period before the Maccabees recaptured the temple and it was ceremonially purified. As mentioned previously, these events foreshadow the actions of the future antichrist (described in verse 36 and onward, which we will address in a later chapter).

The Results of the Vision

The outcomes of this incredible section of prophecy related to the Jewish people serve as a witness to the veracity of God's Word. As highlighted previously, the Dead Sea Scrolls demonstrate that, by 200 BC, the book of Daniel was already an established religious document among the ancient Qumran people (likely of the Jewish religious sect known as the Essenes) and had already been copied many times over. In other words, it is clear that the book of Daniel was present long before the oldest of the Dead Sea Scrolls duplications. It is important to note that some of the prophecies we just detailed above occurred after the Dead Sea Scrolls were produced, serving as yet-future prophecies for those very scribes.

God is a master at giving us just enough evidence to be confident that his Word is true, yet at the same time leaving us with just enough mystery that faith is still required to believe in him. Hebrews 11:6 aptly states, "Without faith it is impossible to please God, because anyone who comes to him must believe that he exists and that he rewards those who earnestly seek him."

Faith is necessary to place our trust in Christ and in God's Word. It also takes faith to follow him. But it is not a blind faith or a mindless faith. It is faith based on reason and evidence. This is important to keep in mind as we study these sweeping prophecies from the book of Daniel.

Now that we have discussed the apologetic nature of the fulfilled prophecies found in the book of Daniel, let's turn our attention to the yet-future prophecies from Daniel's visions, which involve key details about the time of the end.

SECTION 3:

YET-FUTURE PROPHECY

SECTION 1:	SECTION 2:	SECTION 3:	SECTION 4:
HIS-STORY	FULFILLED PROPHECY	YET-FUTURE PROPHECY	APPLICATION

As I'm sure you have noticed by now, the book of Daniel is a complex book that has greater depth than simply the frequently told narratives of the fiery furnace and the lions' den. My purpose for dividing this book into the sections that I have is to direct your thought processes a bit. First, I want to demonstrate God's sovereignty through the historical narrative found in the book of Daniel. Second, I want to highlight the apologetic nature of the 100 percent accuracy rate found in the fulfilled prophecies of the book. Now, I would like to turn our attention to the prophecies of Daniel that remain unfulfilled in our time.

If God is sovereign through history and he predicted all fulfilled prophecy accurately, then we can rightfully conclude that all yet-unfulfilled prophecy will come to pass exactly as predicted in Scripture, and this would include the prophecies of Daniel.

If fulfilled prophecy is evidence that the Bible is indeed the Word of God, then nothing that God predicts for the future should shock or surprise us. Only God can accurately predict the future. His fulfilled prophecies were fulfilled literally. Therefore, we can trust that the yet-future prophecies will also be fulfilled literally. His track record proves his ability to keep his word. All that God has foretold for the future will come to pass. We can bank on it. With that in mind, let's finally turn our attention to the thrilling prophecies from the book of Daniel that foretell events and details related to the time of the end.

CHAPTER 11

The Beast Kingdom

The four great beasts are four kings that will rise from the earth. But the holy people of the Most High will receive the kingdom and will possess it forever—yes, for ever and ever.

DANIEL 7:17-18

We are here.

DANIEL

1 2 3 4 5 6 7 8 9 10 11 12

HISTORICAL NARRATIVE   PREDICTIVE PROPHECY

If you'll recall from our discussion in chapter 8, when we compared the statue from Nebuchadnezzar's dream (Daniel 2) with Daniel's vision of the four beasts (Daniel 7), those prophetic symbols were very clearly pointing to the four successive Gentile empires of Babylon, Medo-Persia, Greece, and Rome. Both of those prophecies include end-times components, predicting key details about what will occur during the future tribulation period. We will discuss these components in this chapter.

In the statue dream from Daniel 2, the feet and toes of the awesome statue are described as an unstable combination of strong iron and weak clay (as is used in pottery). The antichrist's kingdom will be brutally strong, like the Roman Empire, but will not have internal unity, leaving it very brittle. The symbolism present in the feet and the toes is that, though you can combine iron with baked clay, they remain separate materials; the union of the two will not hold up very well.

Most dispensational expositors (those applying a literal approach to interpreting prophecy) agree that the feet and toes together represent the future kingdom of antichrist, and that the ten toes signify the ten elite leaders out of which the antichrist will arise. Chronologically speaking, this fits the model because the rock uncut by human hands will strike both the feet and the toes.

Many experts cite the current state of the European Union as the foundation for this future kingdom. Together, the member nations of the EU are a powerhouse in world politics, but they do not display true, internal unity.

In Daniel's vision of the four beasts, the fourth kingdom is seen as significantly different than the previous three kingdoms. As mentioned previously, the fourth empire is undoubtedly the Roman Empire. In Daniel chapter 7, the Roman Empire is described in the context of its final end-times form. God knows the beginning from the end, and he highlights the worst form the final Gentile empire takes. We read,

> In my vision at night I looked, and there before me was a fourth beast—terrifying and frightening and very powerful. It had large iron teeth; it crushed and devoured its victims and trampled underfoot whatever was left. It was different from all the former beasts, and it had ten horns (verse 7).

I believe that the last phrase, "and it had ten horns," is purposefully placed at the end of this description. After the rapture of the church, the resulting instability will create the perfect scenario for a global government that is run by a small number of elite leaders to emerge from the chaos. We're seeing a push for this even in our day, as the tribulation period casts its shadows ahead of itself.

Daniel 2 refers to these ten leaders as ten toes. Daniel 7 describes them as ten horns. In Revelation 17, they are also called ten horns (verse 7). In that passage, we are told specifically that these will be ten elite end-times rulers, who will assist the antichrist during the future tribulation period (verses 12-13).

Keep in mind, the rapture does not initiate the beginning of the tribulation period; the confirming of a covenant by the antichrist will do this. (We'll discuss that in the next two chapters.) I also should point out that the rapture is not depicted in either Daniel 2 or Daniel 7. It was a mystery revealed in the New Testament. It is very likely that the current arrangement of nations—particularly in Europe—is what is moving history toward the iron and clay feet of the statue.

The Roman Empire was the final empire of the Gentile kings, and it slowly broke apart into nation-states, which are still in the form of Roman-style government and culture. This is the perfect setup for the feet and toes of Daniel chapter 2. The stage seems to be so thoroughly set that the curtain that stands before all end-times events could be lifted at any moment. We await the rapture of the church, which will be the key domino that sets everything into motion.

Dissecting the Toes

The ten toes will be ten elite rulers from a revived Roman Empire, who will rule for a short time with the antichrist. The ten horns described in Daniel 7:24 and Revelation 17:12 support this idea by the interpretations provided in both visions.

I believe we can know for certain that the church will be raptured prior to the antichrist coming to power (2 Thessalonians 2:6-8) and the beginning of the future seven-year tribulation period (Daniel 9:27). It stands to reason that the ten kings rise to power after the rapture. In my mind, it makes most sense that they will not have this opportunity until the rapture has taken place.

The Fifth Kingdom

As we've established, the ten toes are ten kings (elite rulers of some sort) from the geographic area of the Roman Empire. The divine rock is clearly Jesus and his millennial kingdom that will destroy the final world empire (Revelation 20:4). Then his kingdom will become a mountain (Daniel 2:35) permanently overarching everything (the eternal state spoken of in Revelation 21). The more one observes the details of this prophecy, the more mind-blowing it becomes. As we compare scripture with scripture, the more cohesion and unity we discover in the pages spanning from Genesis to Revelation.

In the Daniel 2 prophecy, when the stone strikes only the feet, the entire statue is destroyed. So to recap, we can expect that an evolved or revived yet unstable Roman Empire of sorts will be in place before ten elite rulers will form the final end-times configuration of the fourth kingdom.

At that time, Jesus will return, thus ending the succession of Gentile world empires. He will then usher in the fifth and final empire— the millennial kingdom.

As we've seen in previous chapters, the Old Testament contains many specific prophecies about a literal future kingdom on earth, in which a descendant of David (Jesus) will rule the entire world. Recalling the kingdom context of the book of Daniel, we can see that after the Gentile kingdoms have run their course, finally, this future kingdom will arrive.

In Revelation, the final book of the Bible, we learn details about the earth's final kingdom, such as its duration. In some Christian circles, the details of this future period are allegorized to represent the church age. That would call for a switch in our interpretation method, but there is no reason to have to do that here. In Revelation 20, we are told very plainly that the future kingdom age will last 1,000 years.

Just to make sure we didn't miss the point, John mentions this period a total of six times in the span of only seven verses. In Revelation 20:1-7, we read:

> I saw an angel coming down out of heaven, having the key to the Abyss and holding in his hand a great chain. He seized the dragon, that ancient serpent, who is the devil, or Satan, and bound him for a thousand years. He threw him into the Abyss, and locked and sealed it over him, to keep him from deceiving the nations anymore until the thousand years were ended. After that, he must be set free for a short time. I saw thrones on which were seated those who had been given authority to judge. And I saw the souls of those who had been beheaded because of their testimony about Jesus and because of the word of God. They had not worshiped the beast or its image and had not received its mark on their foreheads or their hands. They came to life and reigned with Christ a thousand years. (The rest of the dead did not come to life until the thousand years were ended.) This is the first resurrection. Blessed and holy are those who share in the first resurrection. The second death has no power over them, but they will be priests of God and of Christ and will reign with him for a thousand years. When the thousand years are over, Satan will be released from his prison.

The plain sense of this passage informs us that the 1,000 years that John describes will take place after tribulation-era believers will have refused to take the mark of the beast. It also tells us that Satan will be bound for the 1,000-year period. If the 1,000-year period when Satan is imprisoned in the abyss is merely allegorical and occurs during the church age, then Satan must have a pretty long chain, based upon all the evil damage he has accomplished since the establishment of the church.

With that backdrop in mind, let's pivot back to the book of Daniel and take a fresh look at Daniel 2 and 7. In Daniel 2:34-35, we read:

> While you were watching, a rock was cut out, but not by human hands. It struck the statue on its feet of iron and clay and smashed them. Then the iron, the clay, the bronze, the silver and the gold were all broken to pieces and became like chaff on a threshing floor in the summer. The wind swept them away without leaving a trace. But the rock that struck the statue became a huge mountain and filled the whole earth.

Fortunately for us, we are given a clear interpretation of the above passage in verses 44-45:

> In the time of those kings, the God of heaven will set up a kingdom that will never be destroyed, nor will it be left to another people. It will crush all those kingdoms and bring them to an end, but it will itself endure forever. This is the meaning of the vision of the rock cut out of a mountain, but not by human hands—a rock that broke the iron, the bronze, the clay, the silver and the gold to pieces. The great God has shown the king what will take place in the future. The dream is true and its interpretation is trustworthy.

The messenger sent to interpret Daniel's vision in Daniel 7 included the following in his description of the coming of the final kingdom:

> Then the sovereignty, power and greatness of all the kingdoms under heaven will be handed over to the holy people of the Most High. His kingdom will be an everlasting kingdom, and all rulers will worship and obey him (Daniel 7:27).

This perfectly mirrors Revelation. We find that the 1,000-year kingdom (Revelation 20:1-7) is followed by the final judgment of Satan and humanity (20:10-15), and then the eternal state (Revelation 21:1–22:5). As the kingdoms of the world wind down, we can anticipate the fifth and final kingdom—the millennial kingdom of Jesus Christ, which serves as merely an overture to eternity with God in heaven.

CHAPTER 12

The Beast of the Kingdom

I also wanted to know about the ten horns on its head and about the other horn that came up, before which three of them fell—the horn that looked more imposing than the others and that had eyes and a mouth that spoke boastfully. As I watched, this horn was waging war against the holy people and defeating them, until the Ancient of Days came and pronounced judgment in favor of the holy people of the Most High, and the time came when they possessed the kingdom.

DANIEL 7:20-22

In the previous chapter, we looked at the future beast kingdom—the worldwide kingdom that will exist during the seven-year tribulation period. Well, this future kingdom of the beast is referred to as such because a beast will run the kingdom. In this chapter, we'll study the various passages in the book of Daniel that provide insight into this evil end-times ruler. He is commonly referred to as the antichrist. Although this term shows up only in the New

Testament—three times in 1 John (2:18, 22; 4:3) and once in 2 John (1:7)—it aptly describes this evil future ruler. He is *anti* in two ways. He will be against Christ, and he will attempt to mimic, counterfeit, or replace Christ.

This evil future ruler will fool the world into believing he is a political messiah—someone who can bring order out of the chaos that will follow the rapture. He will confirm a seven-year treaty with the Jewish people, but near the midpoint of this period he will receive a deadly head wound (Zechariah 11:17; Revelation 13:3), then be brought back to life, it appears, via demonic possession by Satan himself (Revelation 13:1-4). My friend and fellow author Jeff Kinley calls the antichrist "the Devil with skin on." Satan also possessed Judas, the disciple who betrayed Jesus at his first coming (see Luke 22:3; John 13:27).

WHO IS THE ANTICHRIST?

"the little horn"	**Daniel 7:8**
"a fierce-looking king"	**Daniel 8:23**
"a master of intrigue"	**Daniel 8:23**
"the ruler who will come"	**Daniel 9:26**
"a contemptible person"	**Daniel 11:21**
"a shepherd who will not care"	**Zechariah 11:16**
"a worthless shepherd"	**Zechariah 11:16-17**
"man of lawlessness"	**2 Thessalonians 2:3**
"the lawless one"	**2 Thessalonians 2:8-9**
"the rider on the white horse"	**Revelation 6:2**
"a beast"	**Revelation 13:1**

Daniel and Revelation contain more information regarding this evil end-times ruler than any other books of the Bible. The foundational details that inform all the other passages on the topic of the antichrist are found in the visions that Daniel recorded in his book. I often refer to the book of Daniel as the Revelation of the Old Testament. It provides the framework for all other end-times passages in Scripture—including the book of Revelation. In Daniel, the evil end-times ruler is referred to as the little horn (8:9-14; 23-27 ESV) and the king who exalts himself (11:36-45).

The Introduction of the Antichrist

The book of Daniel provides the most complete picture of the antichrist found in the Old Testament. I use this pop-culture term *antichrist* because it is familiar to most, although this term is not found in the book of Daniel, nor in the book of Revelation. As noted above, the evil end-times ruler is referred to as the antichrist only in the books of 1 and 2 John. In reading the passages of Scripture included in the chart above, we learn about this individual and several of his titles, but *antichrist* seems to have become the term that encapsulates them all.

I John 2:18—Dear children, this is the last hour; and as you have heard that the antichrist is coming, even now many antichrists have come. This is how we know it is the last hour.

There are several references to this evil end-times world ruler in the book of Daniel, beginning in chapter 7. In several passages, Daniel describes the evil world leaders who were to come. Then he suddenly jumps into describing the characteristics of the ultimate evil world ruler, who will arise during the time of the end. It's almost as if he's saying, "There are a bunch of evil rulers to come in world history, but none of them will be nearly as horrible as the antichrist. These others simply foreshadow the ultimate evil ruler, who will come to power in the time of the end."

Chapter 7 of Daniel refers to the antichrist as the little horn (verse 8) and gives us some details about his rise to power and some other characteristics. When Daniel asked to be told the meaning of the prophecy, he was given the following information about the antichrist:

> The ten horns are ten kings who will come from this kingdom. After them another king will arise, different from the earlier ones; he will subdue three kings. He will speak against the Most High and oppress his holy people and try to change the set times and the laws. The holy people will be delivered into his hands for a time, times and half a time (verses 24-25).

Then Daniel 8:9-14 provides quite a bit more detail about the evil end-times ruler:

> Out of one of them came another horn, which started small but grew in power to the south and to the east and toward the Beautiful Land. It grew until it reached the host of the heavens, and it threw some of the starry host down to the earth and trampled on them. It set itself up to be as great as the commander of the army of the LORD; it took away the daily sacrifice from the LORD, and his sanctuary was thrown down. Because of rebellion, the LORD's people and the daily sacrifice were given over to it. It prospered in everything it did, and truth was thrown to the ground. Then I heard a holy one speaking, and another holy one said to him, "How long will it take for the vision to be fulfilled—the vision concerning the daily sacrifice, the rebellion that causes desolation, the surrender of the sanctuary and the trampling underfoot of the LORD's people?" He said to me, "It will take 2,300 evenings and mornings; then the sanctuary will be reconsecrated."

Recall in chapter 9 of this book, I highlighted the fulfilled prophecies related to Antiochus Epiphanes and mentioned how this historical figure was also the prototype for the future antichrist. Indeed, during the future tribulation period, the antichrist will follow in the footsteps of Antiochus Epiphanes, but in a much broader and significantly more horrific way. In the Olivet Discourse, Jesus' extensive teaching about the end times (Matthew 24; Mark 13; Luke 21), he describes another yet-future "abomination that causes desolation" (see Matthew 24:15-16; Mark 13:14; Luke 21:20-21). We'll discuss this further in the next chapter.

A careful study and comparison of various passages of Scripture makes it clear that the abomination of desolation will occur at the midpoint of the future seven-year tribulation period, when the antichrist will break his peace agreement with Israel, demand to be worshipped, and persecute the Jewish people (and tribulation-era believers) for the remaining 3.5 years (see Revelation 12:6; 13:5-7).

The second half of the tribulation period is what the passage in Daniel 7:25

was referring to in its description of "the holy people" being "delivered into his hands for a time, times and half a time." This second half of the tribulation is also described as 1,260 days (Revelation 12:6), and as 42 months (Revelation 13:5). Using the Jewish calendar, it is clear these references to time are all speaking of the same period of 3.5 years—the second half of the tribulation period. Daniel 9:27 (which we'll study in the next chapter) highlights the fact that the antichrist will break the covenant in the middle of the seven-year period. Once again, as we compare scripture with scripture, it all lines up perfectly.

Almost 200 years after Antiochus Epiphanes, Jesus spoke of the abomination of desolation as a yet-future end-times event (Matthew 24:15). In the passage, Jesus specifically stated that he was referring to Daniel's prophecy. So, based on the words of Jesus himself, the ultimate fulfillment of the prophecy in Daniel 8:9-14 will occur at the time of the end.

SECOND 1/2 OF THE TRIBULATION PERIOD

1,260 DAYS (REVELATION 12:6)

42 MONTHS (REVELATION 13:5)

3.5 YEARS (DANIEL 9:27)

A TIME, TIMES AND HALF A TIME (DANIEL 7:25)

And in the second part of Daniel chapter 8, we learn even more. The archangel Gabriel unveils additional information about the future antichrist, describing him as "a fierce-looking king" and "a master of intrigue" (verse 23). In verses 24-25, we are told,

> He will become very strong, but not by his own power. He will cause astounding devastation and will succeed in whatever he does. He will destroy those who are mighty, the holy people. He will cause deceit to prosper, and he will consider himself superior. When they feel secure, he will destroy many and take his stand against the Prince of princes. Yet he will be destroyed, but not by human power.

Compare that description of the antichrist with Revelation 12, which describes how Satan will use the antichrist to go after the Jewish people; Revelation 13, which unveils the future mark of the beast; and Revelation 19:11-21, which fills in the details regarding the final stand of the antichrist, when he will foolishly think that he will be able to stand up against Christ at his return.

THE NON-PROPHET'S LATEST BUSINESS VENTURE

The antichrist is also discussed in 2 Thessalonians chapter 2, where he is referred to as the "man of lawlessness." In verses 3-4, we read, "Don't let anyone deceive you in any way, for that day will not come until the rebellion occurs and the man of lawlessness is revealed, the man doomed to destruction. He will oppose and will exalt himself over everything that is called God or is worshiped, so that he sets himself up in God's temple, proclaiming himself to be God."

Paul was specifically talking about the tribulation period (see 2 Thessalonians 2:2), also known as the Day of the Lord—an Old Testament term referring to the time of God's judgment. Paul went on to inform us that the tribulation period will not happen until the rebellion (translated as "apostasy" or "falling away" in other translations) occurs and the antichrist is revealed. As we'll see in the next chapter, he will be revealed by the confirming of a treaty between Israel and others. Then it describes the abomination of desolation, the defiling of the temple.

So you see once again, the Bible fits together like a perfect puzzle! I wish there was one section of Scripture that clearly lays out all the key end-times events in chronological order; however, God sovereignly designed Scripture so that those who really want to understand God's plan for the ages would dig in and study the totality of the canon available to them in their own times. The events of the end concern deep things of God, and they take a bit of study and work to understand. Daniel set an example for us. He set his mind to gain understanding and he humbled himself before his God (see Daniel 10:12). When you look deep, you will see the beauty of Scripture on a much more meaningful level.

Now jumping back to prophecy in the book of Daniel, we also find in chapter 9 that the antichrist will come from the people who will destroy the temple after the death of the Messiah—this destruction was carried out by Rome in AD 70. As I mentioned, he will also confirm or enforce a seven-year covenant with Israel and many other nations, which he will break in the middle of the seven years.

Finally, Daniel chapter 11 contains the last major description of details about the antichrist found in the book of Daniel. We read in 11:36-39,

> The king will do as he pleases. He will exalt and magnify himself above every god and will say unheard-of things against the God of gods. He will be successful until the time of wrath is completed, for what has been determined must take place. He will show no regard for the gods of his ancestors or for the one desired by women, nor will he regard any god, but will exalt himself above them all. Instead of them, he will honor a god of fortresses; a god unknown to his ancestors he will honor with gold and silver, with precious stones and costly gifts. He will attack the mightiest fortresses with the

help of a foreign god and will greatly honor those who acknowledge him. He will make them rulers over many people and will distribute the land at a price.

So, the initial details we gather from the book of Daniel concerning the antichrist are many. And when we view those sections all together, we can paint a fairly clear picture of this individual. Here is a summary of what we can conclude about this future ruler just from the book of Daniel, specifically using the passages listed above. This is the TEPV (Todd's English Paraphrase Version) of key facts about the antichrist, gleaned strictly from Daniel:

Just before the end of the age, when wickedness has greatly increased, a world leader will appear on the scene who will become the most-evil ruler the world has ever known. This fierce-looking and intriguing ruler will most likely arise from somewhere in Western Europe. He will be an elite member of a group of ten rulers. At the beginning of his designated time, he will overtake three of the other rulers and gain power. His strength of position and wild success will not come from his own power, but will be given to him from a greater evil.

The antichrist will complete or enforce some type of treaty with Israel and many other nations. This action will officially begin the seven-year tribulation period (known as Daniel's seventieth "week"). Lies of prosperity will flow from his proud and immoral mouth, and he will break the treaty exactly at the midpoint of its duration. He will all but destroy the world and turn on the Jewish people. He will blaspheme God and successfully and horrifically persecute the Jewish people (and tribulation-era Christians) for three-and-a-half years. He will attempt to change fixed universal properties, such as time and laws.

He will blasphemously portray himself as higher than the one true God. In fact, he will not follow any previous belief system. Instead, he will honor some type of new god—a god of mysterious forces and power (that Satan has unveiled like never before). He will wage war with the help of this "new" god and he will reward anyone who worships him with gifts of position and land ownership.

Finally, this evil leader will even attempt the unthinkable. He will organize a world war against Jesus himself. But this attempted direct assault against the Prince of princes will be the antichrist's complete undoing. His wild and evil success will end in his utter and complete failure. He will be supernaturally defeated and punished.

We learn more details about the antichrist in other areas of the Bible, but it all begins here. These are the foundational facts about this future evil world ruler—all found in the book of Daniel.

Pin the Tail on the Antichrist?

Today, it seems that every time you turn around, there is someone who is pointing at a possible contender who they think could be the antichrist. The passages in 1 and 2 John make it very clear that the spirit of antichrist was already present in the world during the first century AD, so it should be no surprise to us that in every generation since then, there have been those who embody this spirit.

But 2 Thessalonians 2:6-10 provides some key information, reminding us that nobody will know who the antichrist is until after the church (every true believer) is removed via the rapture. In this amazing passage, we read:

> Now you know what is holding him back, so that he may be revealed at the proper time. For the secret power of lawlessness is already at work; but the one who now holds it back will continue to do so till he is taken out of the way. And then the lawless one will be revealed, whom the Lord Jesus will overthrow with the breath of his mouth and destroy by the splendor of his coming. The coming of the lawless one will be in accordance with how Satan works.

He will use all sorts of displays of power through signs and wonders that serve the lie, and all the ways that wickedness deceives those who are perishing.

The Holy Spirit works uniquely in the church age, in that he is said to indwell each true believer (1 Corinthians 3:16). In the moment when the rapture takes place, the salt and light of the world—that preserves righteousness and shines light on unrighteousness—will be removed, then the darkness necessary for the antichrist to rise to power will be present and will allow him to be revealed. Although we see the spirit of antichrist so prevalently in our day, it is useless to try to identify who the antichrist is prior to the rapture of the church.

Now that we have filled in the gaps related to who this evil end-times ruler will be and what will lead to his rise out of the ten kings, let's turn our attention to the single most important prophecy in the book of Daniel.

CHAPTER 13

The 70 Weeks of Years

As soon as you began to pray, a word went out, which I have come to tell you, for you are highly esteemed. Therefore, consider the word and understand the vision.

DANIEL 9:23

If you'll recall our discussion about Daniel chapters 2 and 7 and how they represent the succession of Gentile empires from Daniel's time until the time of the end, you may have wondered to yourself, *What about the Jewish people and their history, from Daniel's time until the time of the end?* Well, that is the topic of Daniel 9, and it is one of the most important prophecies in all of Scripture!

Daniel would have been in his eighties as he was reading Jeremiah's prophecy (Jeremiah 25:1-11), which stated God's chosen people would be in captivity for 70 years before returning home (Daniel 9:1-2). Daniel was concerned for his people and the capital city of Jerusalem, so he set out to fast and pray once again. As usual, God heard Daniel's prayer and gave him more than he bargained for. Not only did God send the angel Gabriel to answer Daniel's prayer about the fulfillment of Jeremiah's prophecy of 70 years of captivity, but he also answered Daniel's prayer regarding a period that was seven times 70 years!

God often works exponentially. He is a God of multiplication. His plans are always greater than ours. So in Daniel 9, the prophet received a 490-year vision—with a long, mysterious gap separating the first 483 years and the final seven years!

Picture this prophecy running parallel to the sweeping prophecies of the Gentile kingdoms. The two prophetic timelines are on separate tracks that are set to come together at the end of the future tribulation period.

The Seventy "Weeks"

This key prophetic theme found in Daniel 9 is known as the 70 weeks (of years). This chapter and particularly the last four verses are absolutely critical to understanding end-times theology. There is so much packed into these four verses that it's like picking up a tennis ball and finding that it weighs as much as a cannon ball. If you don't study anything else in this chapter, I would encourage you to spend time getting a grip on this section. Let's begin by reading Daniel 9:24-27, and I would encourage you to read through it a few times before continuing to the commentary below.

> Seventy "sevens" are decreed for your people and your holy city to finish transgression, to put an end to sin, to atone for wickedness, to bring in everlasting righteousness, to seal up vision and prophecy and to anoint the Most Holy Place.

> Know and understand this: From the time the word goes out to restore and rebuild Jerusalem until the Anointed One, the ruler, comes, there will be seven "sevens," and sixty-two "sevens." It will be rebuilt with streets and a trench, but in times of trouble. After the sixty-two "sevens," the Anointed One will be put to death and will have nothing. The people of the ruler who will come will destroy the city and the sanctuary. The end will come like a flood: War will continue until the end, and desolations have been decreed. He will confirm a covenant with many for one "seven." In the middle of the "seven" he will put an end to sacrifice and offering. And at the temple he will set up an abomination that causes desolation, until the end that is decreed is poured out on him.

At the beginning of Daniel 9, we find Daniel studying Bible prophecy himself. Based on the prophecies of Jeremiah, Daniel understood that the Jewish captivity in Babylon was to last 70 years. Most of chapter 9 records Daniel's prayer to the Lord, in which he confessed his sins and the sins of his people and reminded God of his promises to his people and to his holy city—Jerusalem.

During this prayer, Gabriel the messenger angel—the same angel who would later appear to Zechariah and Mary in the Gospel accounts—appears, and he has an incredibly broad prophecy for Daniel. Daniel's prayer simply inquired about the

end of Jewish exile, and in response God sent a prophecy, through Gabriel, that was much broader in scope and covered all of Jewish history!

The context provided by Daniel praying about the 70 years of Jewish captivity gives us the first hint that the 70 "sevens" is referring to "sevens of years." In other words, 70 sets of seven years. The second hint is the accuracy of those years in relation to the fulfilment of prophecy, which we will look at below. This confirms that 70 sets of seven years is exactly what was meant by the angel Gabriel. So, the full time frame in view here is 490 years (using the Jewish lunar [360-day] calendar that was in place at the time this prophecy was given).

The Full Scope of Jewish History

The foundational statement in this prophecy gives us the full scope. Notice that the 70 "sevens" were decreed, or inexorably planned, for Daniel's people and Daniel's holy city. In other words, this prophecy is fixed, exact, and unchangeable. Daniel was Jewish. The holy city of the Jewish people was and is Jerusalem. This prophecy is specifically for the Jewish people.

The Six Purposes of the Prophecy

If the first statement of the prophecy provides the *what*, then the next statement provides the *why*. There are six purposes of the 70-week time frame. The first three are "to finish transgression, to put an end to sin," and "to atone for wickedness." These refer to Christ's atoning work on the cross and find their ultimate fulfillment at the end of the tribulation period when Christ returns, putting a complete end to sin and when all surviving Jews finally turn to him for salvation.

Another purpose is to "bring in everlasting righteousness." This is clearly a reference to the millennial kingdom, where no evil will be tolerated, and then ultimately, to the final eternal state, where no evil or sin will exist.

The last two purposes are to "seal up vision and prophecy" and to "anoint the Most Holy Place." By the end of this designated time frame, every single prophecy about the Jewish people will have been fulfilled, and Christ himself will purify the temple in Jerusalem.

The Timing of the Messiah's Arrival Foretold

The next phrase in the prophecy is incredible. It provides the exact time frame for the arrival of the Messiah. Just as Daniel relied on Jeremiah's prophecy to know the length of the Jewish captivity, Jews (from the timing of this prophecy, forward) could rely on this "70 weeks" prophecy to understand the timing of the arrival of their long-awaited Messiah. Interestingly, this passage in Daniel is the only place in the Old Testament where Christ is referred to as "Messiah."

This section of the prophecy gives us two historical markers and a specific time frame between them. It tells us that there will be 69 sets of seven years, or 483 years on the Jewish calendar, between a call to "rebuild Jerusalem" and the arrival of the "Anointed One."

We know from Nehemiah 2:1, that in 444 BC, King Artaxerxes allowed Nehemiah to go and rebuild Jerusalem, beginning with the walls around the city. Nehemiah also informs us that this happened in the month of Nisan in the twentieth year of Artaxerxes. Long story short, many believe we can identify this exact date based on historical and archeological records (and if not the exact date, certainly, an accurate time frame). From that point forward, Jews could begin to count the 483 years to the arrival of the Messiah.

This time frame culminates in the spring of AD 33, the time of Jesus' triumphal entry on Palm Sunday, and his crucifixion a few days later. As I alluded to above, many credible prophecy experts have taken the time to calculate all the dates and study the historical references that back up the specific year identified in Nehemiah 2 to make an extremely strong case that this prophecy of 483 Jewish years was fulfilled to the exact day![16] This is why, in Luke 19:42, Jesus said, "If you, even you, had only known *on this day* what would bring you peace—but now it is hidden from your eyes." It is not mere coincidence that the decree to rebuild the city and the walls took place 483 years before the time frame of the events surrounding Jesus' crucifixion.

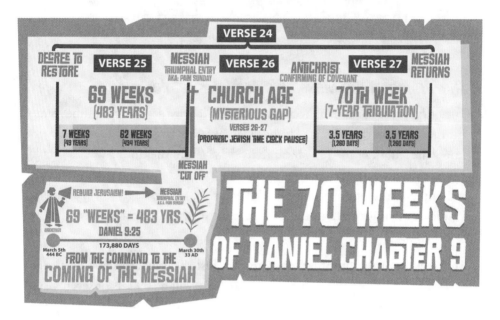

Messiah's Death Prophesied

After the 62 "sevens," the Anointed One will be put to death and will have nothing. This was clearly fulfilled at the cross, where Jesus died. He literally owned nothing and had to be buried in a borrowed tomb. All seemed lost—at least until the resurrection!

The Destruction of Jerusalem and the Temple in AD 70 Prophesied

The middle of Daniel 9:26 says this: "The people of the ruler who will come will destroy the city and the sanctuary." This is the first clear prophecy about the destruction of Jerusalem and the temple. This occurred in AD 70, at the hand of the Roman leader Titus, who would later become emperor. The Arch of Titus in Rome, which commemorates this event, still stands today. Even during New Testament times, the disciples who were taught directly by Jesus didn't realize this destruction was coming, even though it was prophesied here in Daniel. Jesus told his followers about this coming time in his Olivet Discourse and on other occasions. For example, in Luke 19:41-44, we read:

> As he approached Jerusalem and saw the city, he wept over it and said, "If you, even you, had only known on this day what would bring you peace—but now it is hidden from your eyes. The days will come upon you when your enemies will build an embankment against you and encircle you and hem you in on every side. They will dash you to the ground, you and the children within your walls. They will not leave one stone on another, because you did not recognize the time of God's coming to you."

The Tribulation Period Prophesied

We encounter another mountain-peak prophecy in Daniel chapter 9 with a mysterious gap present in verse 26. This gap is where the church age fits in. A gap is necessary between the two periods mentioned in this passage, but you will miss it if you're not looking for it. Notice that in the sequence of the prophecy, it states that the sanctuary—the temple—will be destroyed. Then, in the very next verse it says (among other things) that the antichrist will defile the temple. So, there is a distinction made between the destruction of one temple in Jerusalem and the presence of another temple that will be defiled by the antichrist during the end times. The temple will need to be rebuilt before the antichrist can defile it. Logic demands the gap. Remember that many prophetic mysteries were concealed (but present) in the Old Testament and revealed in the New Testament.

THE MOUNTAIN PEAKS OF DANIEL 9

FRONT VIEW

SIDE VIEW   CHURCH AGE

REBUILDING OF THE TEMPLE BEFORE MID-POINT OF THE TRIBULATION PERIOD

This section about the tribulation period goes on to describe specific details about what will occur during that time that line up perfectly with Revelation and other prophetic sections of Scripture. We learn here that the antichrist figure will "confirm a covenant" for the final set of "seven" in this prophecy, and that he will break the covenant in the middle of its duration. If you recall, I have mentioned that the tribulation period will not be initiated by the rapture; it will begin at the signing of this Daniel 9:27 covenant. Again, this lines up with other key prophetic passages. This evil ruler has a decreed end, of which we can read about in great detail in the closing chapters of Revelation. Once again, we are given the foundations to understand end-times events in Daniel, and more details are given to us in the book of Revelation—details that fill in the gaps.

Living Between Weeks 69 and 70

Within the mysterious gap between the Messiah's being "cut off" and the beginning of the last set of seven years (the tribulation period) is where we exist now, in the present day. We live in exciting times. It is a period focused on God's salvation for the entire world—the Gentile nations. But when this gap period ends, with the confirmation of the Daniel 9:27 covenant (possibly a final version of an Israeli-Palestinian peace treaty), the final seven years of this prophecy will begin.

I believe the Jewish time clock for the first 483 years paused at the triumphal entry of Jesus on what is commonly referred to as Palm Sunday, and I believe it will resume the moment the pen is lifted at the signing of a peace treaty between Israel and other nations.

I also believe there are clear transitional periods at the beginning and end of the church age. In the book of Acts, we see the early church transition from being primarily Jewish to being primarily Gentile. The end-times church should also see a similar transition, when Gentile believers who put their faith into Jesus after the rapture will be joined by many Jewish people who turn to Christ as well. In the last days, Israel will prosper as a nation again, with many Jews returning to their homeland. Their nation will see cultural, technological, and geopolitical conditions that mirror those described for the future tribulation period. We're seeing developments occur around these conditions today, which would further imply that we are likely in the waning moments of the church age.

Once the church is raptured, God's focus will turn back to the Jewish people (though not exclusively, as God has always made a way for all people to come to him). By the end of the seventieth week of this prophecy, 21 judgments will have fallen upon the world, and a remnant of Jewish survivors will all accept Christ (Romans 11:26), ushering in the physical return of the Lord to earth (Zechariah 12:10-14; Matthew 23:39) to destroy his enemies (Revelation 19:11-21) and set up his millennial kingdom (Revelation 20:1-4), with its headquarters in Jerusalem (Luke 1:32-33)!

God has provided us with a glimpse at his plan for the salvation of the people of Israel here in Daniel 9. This chapter of Daniel is critical to our understanding of Bible prophecy. It serves as our model—seen in Daniel's prayer—to approach the Lord humbly when confessing repentance and seeking an understanding of God's Word and his plans. It records both fulfilled and yet-future prophecies, looking hundreds and even thousands of years forward from the time that they were given. These are the first appearances of prophecies that are expounded upon later in Scripture. And they display God's faithfulness to the Jewish people (and to the world), promising an "everlasting righteousness" in the future. Let this be an encouragement to you today.

CHAPTER 14

The End of Days

As for you, go your way till the end. You will rest, and then at the end of the days you will rise to receive your allotted inheritance.

DANIEL 12:13

Everyone wants to know the answers to two questions: "Where did I come from?" and "Where am I going?" The questions of our origin and our destiny go hand in hand. Animals do not ponder such things. Consideration of these concepts is unique to human beings because we are created in the image of God. We are built for eternity.

Even non-Christians seem to be interested with the circumstances by which the world is going to end. The more chaotic the world becomes, the greater the number of books, movies, TV shows, and newscasts that appear, featuring doomsday predictions and pondering. Apart from God, ultimately, all things are hopeless. With God, ultimately, all things are meaningful and purposeful. The view a person holds to about God and the future greatly impacts their thought patterns, decisions, and outlook—much more than many people realize.

The book of Daniel (along with many other books of the biblical prophets) predicts the end of the world. When people think about the subject of the end times from a Christian perspective, they usually think of the book of Revelation—the capstone of Scripture, which tells in great detail what the end will look like. But as you've seen in this study the book of Daniel was written first and is the key framework for the book of Revelation.

With all the winding prophecies and details provided in Daniel's book, none more specifically focuses on the time of the end as does the second half of chapter 11 and all of chapter 12.

I want to recap a few things I noted in chapter 10 of this book, highlighting fulfilled prophecy in the final chapters of the book of Daniel. Daniel 10–12 describes Daniel's final vision. Chapter 10 details the circumstances leading up to the vision. The first half of chapter 11 contains some of the most rapid-fire, detailed prophecies present in the Bible—all of which were fulfilled during the intertestamental period. Then, from the second half of chapter 11 to the end of Daniel's book, the vision shifts its focus to the distant time of the end.

The mountain peaks of prophecy can be spotted across the mountain range we call the book of Daniel. The focus shifts from near to far, and from far to the even more distant future. The end of chapter 11 gives us some interesting details about the lead up to the battle of Armageddon (see Joel 3:14; Revelation 19:19). And chapter 12 continues the end-times narrative, providing key details about the second half of the seven-year tribulation, the lead up to the millennial kingdom, and the final judgment.

Although the vision spans two chapters, we need to keep in mind that those chapter divisions were not present in the original manuscript. They were placed there later to help readers navigate the text and study it. Daniel 10–12 most appropriately is read together in order to get a full understanding of the context and the flow of the narrative. In this chapter, we'll study Daniel 11:40–12:13, which brings us to the end of Daniel's book.

But before we do that, think about this for a moment. The book of Daniel opens with the historical narrative of his captivity, it predicts a future Messiah, and it ends with the final judgment and eternity. If you think about it the book of Daniel is a microcosm of the Bible itself, which opens with the narrative of humankind's captivity to sin, predicts and records the work of the Messiah, and ends with the final judgment and eternity. God does answer our hearts' deep desire to understand our origin and our destiny. Now let's look at some of the incredible prophecies provided to us in the closing section of Daniel's amazing book!

From Messiah Figure to Brutal Dictator

All dictators start as "Mr. Fix-it" men. Hitler and the Nazis rose to power by promising to lift Germany out of the economic depression and the political feebleness it experienced after World War I. Once Hitler consolidated his power his true colors were revealed, and he became one of the evilest dictators the world has ever known.

In a similar fashion, the future antichrist will begin his tenure as a messiah figure—promising to bring peace and stability to an unstable world. His first prophetic act after rising from the ten global end-times rulers will be to confirm (strengthen or complete) a peace treaty between Israel and many nations. He will begin as a man of peace, as symbolized by the first of the infamous four

horsemen of the apocalypse. He'll have a bow, but no arrow. He will have the power to rule but will appear as a man of peace.

However, he won't fool everyone. An assassination attempt on his life will occur just prior to the midpoint of the tribulation period. Many scholars believe he will literally die (while others believe it will be a faux death). When that happens, he will be literally possessed by Satan. The gloves will come off. The facade will be dropped. He will break his covenant with the Jewish people and defile the temple in fulfillment of the prophecies regarding the abomination of desolation. He will attempt to annihilate the Jewish people and—with the help of the false prophet—will enforce the mark of the beast globally. Then he will even turn against the false prophet. He will want sole control of all things spiritual, economic, political, and military. He will demand to be worshipped as God. Many dictators before him have followed similar patterns, but none to the extent that this final world dictator will exhibit.

Apparently, not all countries will comply once the gloves come off. In Daniel 11:40-45, we read:

> At the time of the end the king of the South will engage him in battle, and the king of the North will storm out against him with chariots and cavalry and a great fleet of ships. He will invade many countries and sweep through them like a flood. He will also invade the Beautiful Land. Many countries will fall, but Edom, Moab and the leaders of Ammon will be delivered from his hand. He will extend his power over many countries; Egypt will not escape. He will gain control of the treasures of gold and silver and all the riches of Egypt, with the Libyans and Cushites [*modern-day Ethiopia and*

Sudan] in submission. But reports from the east and the north will alarm him, and he will set out in a great rage to destroy and annihilate many. He will pitch his royal tents between the seas at the beautiful holy mountain. Yet he will come to his end, and no one will help him (author's note in italics).

Commonly in Scripture, the kings of the North and South refer to Syria and Egypt respectively; however, we're not given any further information here. This may refer to Syria and Egypt here, or it may simply refer to countries that are north and south of Israel. In any case, there will be two kingdoms that will resist the domination of the antichrist. The antichrist will use his military strength to quickly conquer many resisting nations. Revelation 6:4 tells us he will be "given a great sword" (ESV). He will have a strong, Roman-like war machine, yet with modern weaponry. The text notes armament such as "chariots and cavalry," but many expositors draw attention to the fact that Daniel was using language that his audience would understand. For example, when describing the participants of the battles and conquests, he used the names of the realms that existed at the time of writing, not necessarily the terms by which they will be known during the end-times.

As the antichrist campaigns in war, he will receive intel about military forces coming to fight him from the east and the north—presumably from end-times configurations of China and Russia. Everything will come to a head in the land of Israel. The antichrist will muster all his forces. We learn in other parts of Scripture that he will wind up staging his armies in the valley of Megiddo, a large, flat plain where many historic battles have been fought. Napoleon Bonaparte is known to have remarked that it was the best place on earth to stage an army.

In the chronology of end-times events, it is at this point when the sixth bowl judgment, prophesied in Revelation 16:12-14, will take place:

> The sixth angel poured out his bowl on the great river Euphrates, and its water was dried up to prepare the way for the kings from the East. Then I saw three impure spirits that looked like frogs; they came out of the mouth of the dragon, out of the mouth of the beast and out of the mouth of the false prophet. They are

demonic spirits that perform signs, and they go out to the kings of the whole world, to gather them for the battle on the great day of God Almighty.

So, although these armies are converging in the Middle East for various reasons, these demonic spirits will convince them all to combine forces in order to fight Jesus Christ at his return. It sounds crazy, but when you read the book of Revelation carefully, you can understand how the previous 19 judgments will prepare the way for all of this to take place at the time of the sixth bowl judgment, deep into the second half of the future tribulation.

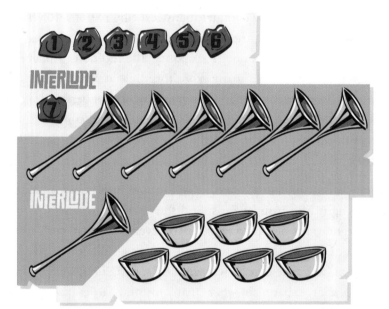

Then will come the final judgment in Revelation—the seventh bowl judgment, which clearly confirms the assessment above. In Revelation 16:16-17, the prophecy continues as we read, "Then they gathered the kings together to the place that in Hebrew is called Armageddon. The seventh angel poured out his bowl into the air, and out of the temple came a loud voice from the throne, saying, 'It is done!'" (see also, Joel 3:14; Revelation 19:19).

Following that simple phrase, "it is done," will come lightning, thunder, and the world's worst earthquake (Revelation 16:18). The next three chapters of Revelation describe the fall of the antichrist's system and, in Revelation 19:11-21, we read about the return of Christ to destroy the armies and throw antichrist and the false prophet into the Lake of Fire. They are the only two humans who will not get to attend the Great White Throne Judgment. Their fate is sealed.

Once again, here the prophetic puzzle pieces from Daniel and Revelation fit together perfectly. Much like a puzzle however, it takes a bit of work to carefully piece it all together. The beauty of Scripture is that you never have to force pieces to fit. You just need to pair the right piece to fit into the correct chronology.

The Time of Jacob's Trouble

Chapter 12 begins by pulling the camera back to reveal further information about the time of the end. The context here is clearly the last 3.5 years of the tribulation (Daniel 12:7). This second half is also known as the time of Jacob's trouble and the great tribulation. It mirrors Revelation 12, which describes a great sign that unpacks what's going on in the spiritual realm during the events on earth as described above. The antichrist's motivation for pursuing and persecuting the Jewish people is unveiled there.

The dragon will go after the Jewish people like a flood, hell-bent on destroying them. Prior to the cross, Satan wanted to eliminate the Jews to prevent the Messiah from coming. Having failed miserably there, through a spirit of antisemitism that brought about events such as the Spanish Inquisition, Russian pogroms, and the Holocaust (just to name a few), throughout the church age Satan has continued in his efforts to destroy them in an attempt to keep Christ from returning.

It is the corporate salvation of a remnant of Jewish people that will usher in the return of Christ (Zechariah 12; 13:8-9; 14:2-3; Matthew 23:39).

This theme is picked up in Daniel 12:1, where we read, "At that time Michael, the great prince who protects your people, will arise. There will be a time of distress such as has not happened from the beginning of nations until then. But at that time your people—everyone whose name is found written in the book—will be delivered."

I may sound like a broken record by now, but once again the puzzle pieces of prophecy fit together perfectly. The verse above is very clearly talking about the Jewish people. Daniel was Jewish. God had established unconditional covenants with the Jewish people (Genesis 12:1-3; 2 Samuel 7:11-13). This is the moment Paul describes in Romans 11:25-27, where he states,

> I do not want you to be ignorant of this mystery, brothers and sisters, so that you may not be conceited: Israel has experienced a hardening in part until the full number of the Gentiles has come in, and in this way all Israel will be saved. As it is written: "The deliverer will come from Zion; he will turn godlessness away from Jacob. And this is my covenant with them when I take away their sins" (see also, Zechariah 13:8-9).

Here we see more mountain peaks of Bible prophecy, when the narrative jumps from the end of the tribulation in Daniel 12:1 to the Great White Throne Judgment in Daniel 12:2-3. We read more details about this time in Revelation 20:11-15, which is the last major event before the eternal state begins. Then as if to say, "The End," the angelic messenger stated to Daniel, "But you, Daniel, roll up and seal the words of the scroll until the time of the end. Many will go here and there to increase knowledge" (Daniel 12:4).

In other words, the prophecies in the book of Daniel will not make much sense for most of history, but as the end of the age approaches they will be unsealed. It appears that this unsealing occurs simultaneously with great advances in travel and human knowledge. With that in mind, consider the following.

Up until around 200 years ago, the fastest way to travel was by using horses. In the year 1825, the first public steam railway was introduced. Humankind didn't fly heavier-than-air machines until December 17, 1903, when Orville Wright successfully flew for a whopping 12 seconds. Since then, we've broken the sound barrier, traveled to the moon and back, set up an international space station, and made worldwide travel easily accessible to just about anyone.

In the mid-twentieth century, the world entered the information age. It marks a significant leap in wide-spread human knowledge thanks to many advances in technology and communication. And yet, as it continues on today, there are so many forms of new knowledge that we can't keep up with them all.

In addition to general human knowledge, many prophecy experts point out that these verses may also indicate that end-times prophecies will be unlocked in the last days. This means that many prophetic passages that historically have not been understood are being unlocked in our generation, resulting in greatly increased prophetic knowledge as we study the Scriptures and consider current events.

Confusing Time Clues

Throughout this study, I've been highlighting how the time frames concerning various passages of Bible prophecy all fit together so perfectly. Seven years are specified for the tribulation to take place in the prophecy in Daniel 9:27. Three and a half years will transpire during the Great Tribulation, when the Jewish people will be on the run. This is also supported by 1,260 days, 42 months, and the phrase "a time, times and half a time." Then we read Daniel 12:11-12, and out of the blue we have some unfamiliar time clues: 1,290 days and 1,335 days. Those periods don't line up with anything else we've studied thus far.

Let's take a look at those verses. We read, "From the time that the daily sacrifice is abolished and the abomination that causes desolation is set up, there will be 1,290 days. Blessed is the one who waits for and reaches the end of the 1,335 days" (Daniel 12:11-12).

Keep in mind, when considering the context of Daniel 12, that this vision is measuring from specific key milestones to the time of the very end. There is no clear indicator elsewhere in Scripture as to why there are an extra 30 days in one time frame and an additional 45 days (75 total) in the other.

What follows is sanctified speculation, but perhaps it will take 30 days after the end of the tribulation for a key aspect of the preparation for the millennial kingdom to take place (perhaps the sheep and goat judgment, or the cleaning and preparation of the temple, or repairing areas of Jerusalem for Christ to rule). And perhaps it will take an additional 45 days for the world to be readied for the official start of the millennial kingdom.

After seven years of horrific judgments—including global war, earthquakes, meteors, volcanic eruptions, poisonous waters, scorching heat, and several other decimating events—it will take time for the earth's landscape to be renovated, for plants to grow, and for the government centers of the millennial kingdom to be set up. In the millennial kingdom, deserts will bloom with flowers (see Isaiah 30:23-24; 35:1-7), topography will be changed (Micah 4:1;

Zechariah 14:9-10; Revelation 16:20), and a literal global government will be set up (Isaiah 9:6-7).

Of Kingdoms and Ages

So as you can see from this study of Daniel, while the Gentile kingdoms have dominated much of history, there is another kingdom theme present. The future millennial kingdom is on its way, which is merely an overture to eternity.

If you have ever been to a symphony or a musical, you may have noticed that it often begins with an overture—a condensed version of the entire performance with parts of music from each scene. This is merely a foretaste of what is to come.

The millennial kingdom is merely an introduction to God's extended work of eternity! It won't be boring. It will be perfect in every sense of the word.

The beauty of the message in both Daniel and Revelation is, that although evil has its day, God is sovereignly at work to bringing about its designated end. Evil will be judged. Restoration will be achieved. The people of God will rule and reign with him—first in the millennial kingdom, then for all eternity. What could be better?

CHAPTER 15

Filling in the Gaps

Jesus left the temple and was walking away when his disciples came up to him to call his attention to its buildings. "Do you see all these things?" he asked. "Truly I tell you, not one stone here will be left on another; every one will be thrown down." As Jesus was sitting on the Mount of Olives, the disciples came to him privately. "Tell us," they said, "when will this happen, and what will be the sign of your coming and of the end of the age?"

MATTHEW 24:1-3

If the book of Daniel provides the main framework for God's plan for the ages, including the end times, then I thought it would be valuable to do a brief overview of two other key sections of Scripture that help fill in some gaps—the Olivet Discourse and the book of Revelation.

If I could use an analogy from the world of cinema, Daniel offers us a wide establishing shot of the forest. While in the Olivet Discourse, Jesus provides a tighter mid-range shot of the trees. Then John, in the book of Revelation, provides a close-up shot of the branches and leaves.

It is very significant that Jesus spoke so often about the end times. Many people do not realize that every one of Jesus' parables recorded in the Gospels are kingdom parables. In other words, they all have an end-times component pointing to the future millennial kingdom.

Out of necessity, those who hold to an amillennialist viewpoint on the end times (they don't believe in a literal future kingdom age) allegorize Scripture anytime Jesus or other writers mention details about a literal future kingdom age. The Lord's Prayer includes the phrase "your kingdom come, your will be done, on earth as it is in heaven" (Matthew 6:10). I believe Jesus was speaking literally, not figuratively.

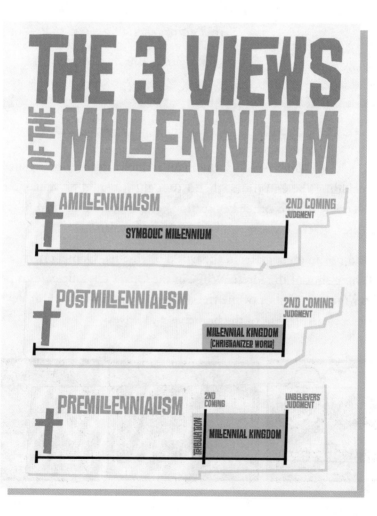

If that is not overt enough, consider Jesus' clear statement in his exchange with Peter found in Matthew 19:27-28, where we read:

> Peter answered him, "We have left everything to follow you! What then will there be for us?"
>
> Jesus said to them, "Truly I tell you, at the renewal of all things, when the Son of Man sits on his glorious throne, you who have followed me will also sit on twelve thrones, judging the twelve tribes of Israel."

The Jewish people at large thought Jesus would soon usher in this literal kingdom prophesied in the Old Testament. That was the whole reason behind his triumphal entry on what we refer to as Palm Sunday. The only problem was that they thought he was merely a political Messiah. They didn't realize that he first came to pay for our sins. When he was subsequently rejected as Messiah by the Jewish leaders and the masses, it showed that it was not time for the Messiah's kingdom era on earth—this was all sovereignly organized by the Father so that Gentiles could be grafted into God's plan (Romans 11:11-31).

Jesus' Olivet Discourse

In addition to Jesus' many parables and other statements related to the end times, his most impactful and direct teaching on the topic is known as the Olivet Discourse. This is a more concise way of saying, "the talk Jesus had with his disciples on the Mount of Olives, near the area of the temple." Aside from the book of Revelation, it contains the longest passage about end-times prophecy in the New Testament. It is also the second-longest continuous teaching of Jesus, the longest being the Sermon on the Mount.

The Olivet Discourse is found in Matthew 24–25, Mark 13, and Luke 21:5-36. No single passage contains every word of Jesus' teaching in the discourse, and each writer focused on different details with their particular audience in mind. A careful comparison of all three accounts provides a more complete view, and the account in Matthew provides the longest version of the teaching.

The entirety of what Jesus spoke about in the discourse was future prophecy. His prophecy about every stone being torn down was fulfilled in exact detail just 34 years after the prophecy was given. Literally every single stone of the temple building was thrown down so that the Romans could access all the gold that had melted between the cracks when the temple had been burned down during their attack on Jerusalem. You can still see many of the large stones lying at the base of the Temple Mount today. We know the rest of Jesus' prophecies will also be fulfilled in exact detail.

Olivet Discourse Mirrors Revelation

There are two views of the Olivet Discourse held to among pretribulational, premillennial, dispensational, futurist scholars. In other words, even among theologians who believe in a literal approach to interpreting prophecy (that future prophecy will literally come to pass just as fulfilled prophecy has come to pass literally), and that the rapture will happen prior to the tribulation period, and that Jesus will return prior to a literal kingdom age on earth, and that God has distinct programs for Israel and the church, which tie together perfectly in the future kingdom age and beyond, there are two views about the nature of the Olivet Discourse.

One camp sees most of the details (other than the abomination of desolation and the literal return of Christ) as church-age prophecies leading up to the rapture. The other camp believes Jesus is talking strictly to a Jewish audience with no reference to the rapture, and that Jesus is talking primarily of events in the future tribulation period.

I used to hold view 1, mainly because it was the first view I bumped into and didn't realize there was another view. But after much study of both views, I have come to conclude that the second option is the correct view. I believe

Jesus was not talking about the rapture or events leading up to the rapture in Matthew 24. I believe he was talking specifically about events in the future tribulation period. There's not enough room in this chapter to explain all the reasons why, but here are a few of the key reasons I hold to that view.

First, Jesus was talking to a Jewish audience and Paul had not yet written his epistles or been given any information about the mystery of the rapture. That would come a few decades later. The rapture is specifically a church-age mystery and the church age did not begin until Pentecost—after Jesus had returned to heaven. In fact, Jesus said the Holy Spirit could not come until he returned to the Father (John 16:7). So at the time of the Olivet Discourse, Jesus' Jewish disciples would have been thinking about the return of Christ to set up the kingdom. They had no knowledge of the rapture.

Second, Jesus' description of signs in Matthew 24:4-8 line up with the first set of sequential judgments in the book of Revelation (deception/false Messiah, war, famine, earthquake). These details mirror the outcome of the first six seal judgments of Revelation 6 perfectly. Jesus said those are the beginnings of birth pains. The six seals are opened during the beginning of the tribulation period.

Third, Matthew 24:9-14 mirrors other details of the tribulation period, then verses 15-28 describe the abomination of desolation, followed by the antichrist's attempt to destroy the Jewish people.

Finally, verses 29-31 point to the return of Christ at the end of the tribulation period. These details all line up with the events and chronology described in Revelation chapters 6–19. So, I see the Olivet Discourse as Jesus' condensed preview of the book of Revelation.

I have great friends who hold to the other view, and we see this as an in-house debate. I would encourage you to do your own study to form your convictions about this passage. As you do, be sure to account for all related scriptures from the Old and New Testaments.

The Revelation from Jesus

It makes sense that the Olivet Discourse would line up with Revelation because they were both revealed by Jesus himself! The Olivet Discourse was Jesus' teaching to his disciples, and in Revelation we are told in the very first verse of the book that it is the revelation from Jesus Christ to the prophet John. John then described (to the best of his ability) the glorified Christ who spoke to him. Following Revelation chapter 1, Jesus himself dictated seven letters to seven churches in Asia Minor (modern-day Turkey). So, you might even call these the seven epistles of Jesus!

For a full study on the book of Revelation, you may want to check out *The Non-Prophet's Guide™ to the Book of Revelation*, where I provide a carefully detailed chronological walk through the book of Revelation from chapter 1 to the end. For the purposes of this chapter, I'll highlight a few examples that show that Revelation helps define key structural details provided in the book of Daniel.

Revelation has one of the simplest structures of any book in the Bible. We are provided with the outline of the book in the first chapter. In Revelation 1:19, we read, "Write, therefore, what you have seen, what is now and what will take place later." There you have your simple outline:

I. Things You Have Seen (Glorified Christ in Heaven—1:12-18)

II. Things Which Are (Direction to the Seven Churches—chapters 2–3)

III. Things That Take Place After (Future/Tribulation/Kingdom/Eternity—chapters 4–22)

There are also specific phrases throughout Revelation demonstrating that it is written primarily in chronological order—phrases like "after this," "when he had opened the seventh seal," "the seven last plagues," and "after these things." These are time-oriented sequential phrases and there is a natural progression and buildup of events throughout the book. We even find that the seal, trumpet, and bowl judgments are each numbered in order, from one through seven.

The only sections that are not in chronological order are chapters 10–14. These are parenthetical, or overview, chapters. They provide more context for some of the broad themes and extended events of the tribulation period. It's almost like an intermission in the middle of the book. After the seal and trumpet judgements, John pauses to provide more context and detail, and to let you catch your breath. Then he picks up again in chapter 15 with the bowl judgments.

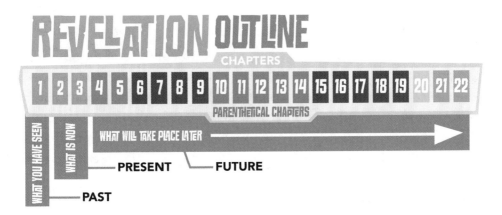

John assumed his readers would be familiar with the Old Testament. In fact, Revelation is a distinctly Jewish book. In it we find all kinds of Jewish symbolism, two Jewish witnesses, 144,000 Jewish evangelists, and the world's attention centered on Israel and Jerusalem in the end times. In Revelation's 404 verses, there are more than 800 references or allusions to the Old Testament! Having read this book up to this point, you are now very acquainted with the prophecies and some of the symbolism in the Old Testament.

The symbolism present in Revelation is understood either by reading the immediate context in which it appears, or by cross-referencing passages from the Old Testament. Many Bible expositors teach what is known as "the law of first mention." To understand the doctrines or symbols used in Revelation, you must find the first place in Scripture that the doctrine or symbol is mentioned. The first instance of a teaching or symbol often provides tremendous insight into how it is to be understood later. Then, cross-referencing all uses of a key word or term will help you to build upon the doctrine or symbol's first mention.

This approach helps us interpret scripture with scripture, instead of interpreting passages based on outside sources or our own thoughts and ideas. If God is the author of the Bible, we should expect to find a cohesiveness in this regard—and we do. The law of first mention, and the principle of interpreting scripture with scripture, both bear out a divine unity in Scripture as it relates to numbers, symbols, doctrines, names, places, and many other details. Using these approaches when studying Revelation helps to bring great clarity to most of its symbolism.

In Revelation 6, we see the tribulation begin with opening of the first seal judgment, which brings the rider on the white horse. If you'll recall, according to Daniel chapter 9, the evil end-times global leader we commonly refer to as the antichrist will confirm a covenant between Israel and many nations. This single event officially starts the ticking down of the seven-year clock until the physical return of Christ to earth to set up the millennial kingdom.

While the tribulation is taking place on earth, the church will experience two beautiful events in heaven. First, we will (as mentioned previously) attend the Bema Seat, or Judgment Seat of Christ to receive rewards for service. Second, we will attend the marriage supper of the Lamb (Revelation 19:6-10). There's one more amazing event you and I as church-age believers will experience, but I'll keep this in chronological order.

With the onset of the tribulation period, the world will go through 21 judgments that go from bad to worse. The effects of the seal judgments will carry into the trumpet judgments and the effects of those will carry into the bowl judgments. Prophecy teachers vary on when the judgments take place. I believe the seal and trumpet judgments will occur during the first 3.5 years of the tribulation, followed by some key midpoint events, then the bowl judgments will occur during the second half of the seven-year period.

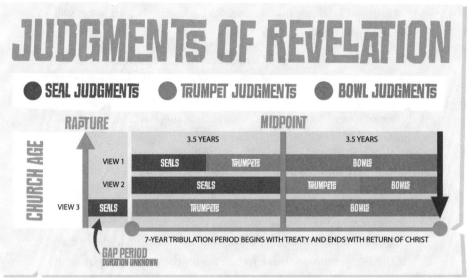

The three main views of tribulation events. I lean (though not dogmatically) toward VIEW 1.

The second half of the tribulation is also known as the great tribulation (Daniel 12:1; Matthew 24:21) or the time of Jacob's (Israel's) trouble (Jeremiah 30:7). Revelation 12 and Matthew 24 highlight various details about when, at the midpoint of the tribulation, Satan and his minions will be cast down to the earth. The enemy will know his time is short and he will go after the Jewish people with everything he has, trying to destroy them. If you'll recall from previous chapters, for exactly 3.5 years, a remnant of Jewish people will be protected in a place prepared for them. It is important to remember that one of the key purposes of the tribulation period is the salvation of the Jewish nation. A remnant will survive the tribulation period (Zechariah 13:8-9), and this is when "all Israel will be saved" (Romans 11:26).

Daniel's Dilemma

Daniel the prophet, who had interpreted prophetic dreams for kings and received visions from Gabriel and other angelic beings, was stumped by the last section of the vision we unpacked in the previous chapter. In Daniel 12:8-10, we read:

I heard, but I did not understand. So I asked, "My lord, what will the outcome of all this be?"

He replied, "Go your way, Daniel, because the words are rolled up and sealed until the time of the end. Many will be purified, made spotless and refined, but the wicked will continue to be wicked. None of the wicked will understand, but those who are wise will understand."

In contrast, when we read Revelation 22:10-11, we see John receives the following direction from an angel (perhaps the same one):

Do not seal up the words of the prophecy of this scroll, because the time is near. Let the one who does wrong continue to do wrong; let the vile person continue to be vile; let the one who does right continue to do right; and let the holy person continue to be holy.

We see that with the close of the canon of Scripture, prophecy has been unsealed. Though Daniel was not given more detail in his time, he was to take heart and remain faithful. In Daniel, many prophecies were concealed. In Revelation, they are revealed (it's even in the name). Again, the book of Daniel, the Olivet Discourse, and the book of Revelation go hand in hand. Daniel, Jesus, and John provided prophecies that all fits in perfect harmony. Both Daniel and John record that the human condition will not get better. Wicked people will remain wicked, and righteous people (those saved by the grace of God) will grow in their faith. Daniel's narrative includes the telling fact that evil people will not understand the times or God's plans, but the righteous will. Evil people scoff at prophecy and are walking blindly. Wise people study it and understand the times!

SECTION 4:

APPLICATION

SECTION 1: HIS-STORY

SECTION 2: FULFILLED PROPHECY

SECTION 3: YET-FUTURE PROPHECY

SECTION 4: APPLICATION

It may surprise you to hear me state that Daniel is one of the most practical books in the Bible. In fact, I would argue that it is more practical now than it has ever been!

Here is what I mean by that. The book of Daniel was practical for its immediate audience at the time of the captivity and the prophesied return of the Jewish people to Jerusalem. It also gave them hope for the future to know that God keeps his promises and had a plan for the future of Daniel's people once the series of Gentile empires had run its course. God had not forgotten them. This helped them maintain their identity from Daniel's time all the way to today.

Yet I say the book of Daniel is even more practical today for several reasons. Here are a few. With the benefit of having the entire Bible—Genesis to Revelation—we can see the full plan of God for the ages, unsealed for us now during the church age. We see how God's unconditional promises to the Jewish people were planned in a way so that Gentiles could believe in the Messiah as well. Genesis 12:1-3 eventually led to John 3:16! Now anyone can come to God through the finished work of Christ. That is why in Galatians 3:28, Paul stated, "There is neither Jew nor Gentile, neither slave nor free, nor is there male and female, for you are all one in Christ Jesus."

Paul wasn't implying there that the church had replaced Israel. He was simply stating that we are all one in Christ. God's plans for Israel's future still stand. Paul says plainly, "I ask then: Did God reject his people? By no means!" (Romans 11:1). Later in verse 29 of the same chapter, he elaborates further when he states, "God's gifts and his call are irrevocable." In other words, God is a promise keeper. He will always finish what he has started and will always honor his word. God has two distinct (but related) programs—one for Israel, and one for the church.

So, we understand the full plan of God. We also have demonstrable proof that the Bible is from God. The plethora of fulfilled prophecies present in the book of Daniel can only be explained by the fact that it must be divine in nature. Only someone who is outside of time and knows the future can predict with pinpoint accuracy the numerous prophecies within this single book of the Bible.

The book of Daniel is also practical for us today because we are living in an increasingly pagan, godless culture, where the likelihood of facing persecution increases daily. As we study the life of Daniel and the stands that he and his friends took, we can know that God will guide us through our times as we stand for righteousness and continue to serve the Lord with passion and purpose.

Lastly, the book is practical from a prophetic standpoint because we are closer now than ever before to the events spoken of by Daniel. The careful student of the book of Daniel can see the seventieth week approaching! The tribulation period casts its shadow ahead as we witness prophetic developments in our day like no other time in history.

So in this final section, I want us to turn our attention to discovering some personal application from the book of Daniel. I don't want this study to merely be an intellectual pursuit, but one that causes us to grow spiritually so that we can be prepared for what is ahead and be used by God in our generation.

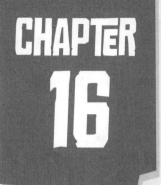

CHAPTER 16

Starting Point

Shadrach, Meshach and Abednego replied to him, "King Nebuchadnezzar, we do not need to defend ourselves before you in this matter. If we are thrown into the blazing furnace, the God we serve is able to deliver us from it, and he will deliver us from Your Majesty's hand. But even if he does not, we want you to know, Your Majesty, that we will not serve your gods or worship the image of gold you have set up."

DANIEL 3:16-18

Daniel and his three friends stood for the Lord in tough times. Their successful navigation through the tough reality they were facing and their dedication to God all started with one thing—a relationship with the Lord.

If you are reading this and recognizing that you still have not opened your heart to the loving Savior who died for you, now is the time, and here is the way. It's not a formula or a legalistic step of action. It's not based on works in any shape or form. Becoming a Christian is simply believing in Jesus for salvation. It's one thing to believe facts *about* Jesus. It's an entirely different thing to believe *in* Jesus. I can believe a chair will hold me, but I need to sit in the chair to express real faith. You can tell someone you want to marry them, but it's an entirely different thing to walk down the aisle and say, "I do."

In previous chapters, I have mentioned various epistles written by the apostle Paul, particularly Romans 11, about God's continued plans for the Jewish people. Romans is a theological treasure trove. It is like the theological handbook of the New Testament. In it, Paul explains salvation in very clear terms.

Over time, evangelists, pastors, and missionaries have selected verses from the book of Romans to share the message of salvation with others in an easy-to-understand way. This has come to be known as the Romans Road to Salvation.

The Need

Romans 3:23—"All have sinned and fall short of the glory of God."

The Consequences of Sin

Romans 6:23—"The wages of sin is death…"

God's Solution/Provision

Romans 6:23—"…but the gift of God is eternal life in Christ Jesus our Lord."

Romans 5:8—"God demonstrates his own love for us in this: While we were still sinners, Christ died for us."

How to Receive Salvation

Romans 10:9-10—"If you declare with your mouth, 'Jesus is Lord,' and believe in your heart that God raised him from the dead, you will be saved. For it is with your heart that you believe and are justified, and it is with your mouth that you profess your faith and are saved."

The Guarantee of Salvation

Romans 10:13—"Everyone who calls on the name of the Lord will be saved."

The Results of Salvation

Romans 5:1—"Since we have been justified through faith, we have peace with God through our Lord Jesus Christ."

Romans 8:1—"There is now no condemnation for those who are in Christ Jesus."

The Protection of Salvation

Romans 8:38-39—"I am convinced that neither death nor life, neither angels nor demons, neither the present nor the future, nor any powers, neither height nor depth, nor anything else in all creation, will be able to separate us from the love of God that is in Christ Jesus our Lord."

That helps lay it all out, but it is only knowledge unless you make this real in your life. Receiving Christ is an intentional decision. You control the doorknob. Christ is knocking at the door and wants to come in (Revelation 3:20). The question is, will you let him? I promise you that receiving him as Savior will be the best decision of your life. If you want to do that, here's a simple way to make it happen.

While some topics in Scripture are complex and take much study to understand, the concept of salvation is simple enough for a child to understand. In fact, it's as simple as A, B, C.

Admit that you are a sinner. None of us are perfect. We all fall short. Romans 3:23: "All have sinned and fall short of the glory of God." Romans 6:23: "The wages [payment] of sin is death, but the gift of God is eternal life in Christ Jesus our Lord."

Believe that Jesus is God's Son and that he died on the cross with your sins on him. Romans 5:8: "While we were still sinners, Christ died for us."

Confess him as your Lord. This doesn't mean you will never mess up again. Rather, it means you will serve him and learn his ways as you grow spiritually. Romans 10:9: "If you confess with your mouth the Lord Jesus and believe in your heart that God has raised Him from the dead, you will be saved" (NKJV).

Accepting Christ also involves repentance. Repentance means making a mental U-turn. It means you agree with God's Word about sin. To walk with the Lord is to walk in agreement with him.

Here's a simple prayer you can pray. These words aren't magic. Again, this is not a formula. But if these words accurately reflect the motives of your heart, then when you pray this prayer, you will become a Christian. You will have placed your faith in Christ and will have had your sins forgiven. You will look forward to an eternity with Jesus in heaven, and you will avoid the terrible time of tribulation that will soon come to the world. Pray this prayer now:

> Lord Jesus, I admit that I am a sinner. I have sinned against you, and sin separates me from you. I thank you that you died on the cross for me. You took my sins upon you and paid my penalty at the cross. I believe you are who you say you are—God in the flesh. I believe you died for my sins. I want to accept your gift of salvation and, at this moment, I ask you to be my Savior. I thank you for this great forgiveness. I now have new life. I now claim you as my Savior and my Lord. In Jesus' name, amen.

If you just genuinely prayed the spirit of that prayer, you are a new creation. The Bible tells us that heaven is celebrating right now because of your decision.

The Holy Spirit now indwells you and will guide you and keep you. You won't be perfect, but you are forgiven, and God will never leave you. His work in you has just begun. You are an adopted co-heir with Christ. You will one day live and reign with him in the millennial kingdom and forever in eternity. Welcome to the family of God!

So, what's next for you on your journey? There is one critical practice that Daniel modeled for all believers. It is life changing and of utmost importance. It is key to living the Christian life successfully as we navigate the many pitfalls of our times. Turn the page to find out what it is!

CHAPTER 17

Practicing Daniel's Pattern of Prayer

Let us then approach God's throne of grace with confidence, so that we may receive mercy and find grace to help us in our time of need.

HEBREWS 4:16

Do you wonder about what made Daniel so different? What made him a prime candidate for God to use him in such immense ways? From knowing and interpreting the prophetic dream of a pagan king to receiving direct revelation from divine beings about Jewish and Gentile history from his time all the way into eternity, Daniel was used by God in an incredible way. Sometime early on, Daniel had dedication to the Lord and commitment to prayer modeled for him. Sometime early on, Daniel made a decision that would change the trajectory of his life. Young Daniel made a conscious decision to follow the God of Abraham, Isaac, and Jacob into the unknown without reservations.

And he's not the only one. Think of Joseph, who was betrayed by his brothers and sold into slavery as a teenager. In Genesis, we read that he faced hardships over and over again yet he chose to

187

submit himself to the purposes and the timing of the Lord, and God used him to save God's people and bless them in immense ways. Or in the New Testament, think of Mary, the mother of Jesus. She was another young, godly teenager who made a conscious choice to be used by God with the attitude of, "I am the Lord's servant" (Luke 1:38).

In the world's eyes, these young teenagers had their lives upended by the purposes of God. Wrecked. But they each saw the bigger picture. They all walked by faith, trusting that God's sovereignty would guide their steps. They were willing to stand for God and walk by faith in the face of immense pressure to take the easy ways out—at least for the short term.

So, what was it that helped them to stand their ground? What gave them such spiritual spines of steel in the face of the great odds against them? Why did God choose to use them in such incredible ways? Why did each of them receive prophetic visitations and dreams from God's holy servants from the unseen realm? These teenagers weren't superheroes. They were regular, everyday human beings. But they were wholly dedicated to the Lord in the quietness of their lives. Character is formed when no one is looking. They had a relationship with the Lord that was cultivated by prayer and dedication.

Dedication is one thing, but how should God's people respond when pressure is applied—when the chips are down, and everything seems stacked against them? In this chapter, I want us to take a look at Daniel's pattern of prayer that sustained him through tough trials and against incredible odds. It was the lifeline that kept him connected to his spiritual power source.

One of the often-overlooked details in the book of Daniel is the incredible model of prayer we're given as we read the narrative. In Daniel chapters 2, 6, 9, and 10, we're given some very detailed play-by-play vignettes of how Daniel prayed in his time of need. As we observe various details of his prayers, there are some very practical things we can apply to our own lives as we face trials and uncertainty. Let's take a look!

Don't Go It Alone

Although we don't do it perfectly, my wife and I pray together regularly and take our things to the Lord. Most of our prayers are short and related to events of the day, things that are on our hearts, and prayers for our daughter, two sons, and daughter-in-law. Occasionally, we're faced with an unexpected life challenge that requires more intense prayer. The greater the need, the more intentional, specific, and desperate our prayers become.

I am also blessed to have a few close friends whom I can be very real with. These are my brothers in Christ. We are soldiers in arms against the very real spiritual warfare that takes place in the life of a dedicated believer. We keep in close contact and often ask each other to pray for specific needs. We spend time together. Our friendship is real and raw because life is real and raw.

In Daniel chapter 2, we see that Daniel had such an approach to prayer during a crisis moment. King Nebuchadnezzar had a dream and was so sick of the pretense of his magicians and wise men that he planned to kill all of them if no one could explain his disturbingly prophetic dream.

Read these verses from Daniel 2, and let the weight of the moment sink in. In verses 12-13, we read:

> This made the king so angry and furious that he ordered the execution of all the wise men of Babylon. So the decree was issued to put the wise men to death, and men were sent to look for Daniel and his friends to put them to death.

What?! Daniel didn't even do anything. And now he's faced with certain death? What Daniel did next was a risky move, but the safest action to take is always to risk everything on God. Daniel put a target on his back by approaching the king. Here is what happened:

Daniel went in to the king and asked for time, so that he might interpret the dream for him. Then Daniel returned to his house and explained the matter to his friends Hananiah, Mishael and Azariah. He urged them to plead for mercy from the God of heaven concerning this mystery, so that he and his friends might not be executed with the rest of the wise men of Babylon. During the night the mystery was revealed to Daniel in a vision (verses 16-19).

Notice Daniel's pattern of prayer in a crisis:

1. *Walk toward the challenge, not away from it.*
   God is sovereign over the confusing and uncertain details of your life.

2. *Carve out time to pray and seek the Lord.*
   Often in crisis, we go right into fix-it mode. We feel like there is not time to pray and that action needs to be taken. Solutions need to be found. But when we do that, we're doing it in our own strength and not the Lord's. Daniel was too busy not to pray! When the pressure is on—that is the time to pray. You will accomplish more on your knees praying than with any other activity. In crisis, we need to postpone decision making until we have heard from the Lord.

3. *Invite others to pray with you.*
   Daniel asked his three friends to pray. They had skin in the game as well. Their lives were on the line. This step has a prerequisite. First, we need to cultivate a few close godly friendships. We must be intentional about this.

4. *Approach God humbly.*
   Notice Daniel urged his friends to plead for God's mercy. They needed God to show up in this situation or they were dead. It was literally a life-or-death answer to prayer they were seeking. The situation was hopeless without God's intervention.

5. *Trust God to show up at just the right time according to his sovereignty.*

Many of our prayers are not answered in the time frame we desire. God has a different timetable. All of the moving parts of our lives are in his view. He is always right on time and never late.

One of the crises my wife and I have faced in our lives was at the birth of our eldest son. He was born with pneumonia. We were totally blindsided. The delivery went well, then as the doctor and nurses were examining him, they immediately noticed that he was not breathing correctly. Without warning he was whisked away to the Newborn Intensive Care Unit (NICU), where he would spend his first week of life outside of the womb. He was born on a Sunday morning, just before church. I called my pastor and asked him to pray with us. At the beginning of the church service that day, he invited everyone there to pray with him for our son.

Two days later when we met with the NICU doctor, he said, "I can't figure it out. His X-rays still look horrible, but he's behaving as if nothing is wrong with him at all. I would let you take him home today, but I recommend we finish his week-long antibiotic treatment and keep a close eye on him." Thank you, Lord!

Fast-forward about five years, and we found ourselves in a similar situation with our youngest son. He briefly stopped breathing while nursing one day, so my wife took him to the doctor, who then sent him to the emergency room. After hours of testing for seizures and other possible explanations, they noticed something on the X-ray of his heart. It appeared he had a heart defect. Another test was ordered for the next day. The situation seemed serious enough that they had a team of doctors from John's Hopkins in Baltimore looking at the real-time results as the test was performed. It just so happened that this test was on Sunday morning—again.

For a second time, we interrupted our pastor's Sunday morning routine to ask for prayer. Yet again, he had the whole church join him as he led in prayer. The test was performed and the lead doctor from John's Hopkins said, "I don't see anything at all that is wrong with his heart. What you saw in the previous test must have been a mistake." Thank you, Lord—again!

Thankfully, both of these crises had incredible endings. I know this is not always the case. It hasn't always been the case with us. We experienced another crisis situation when we lost our son Ethan when my wife was five months pregnant with him. We prayed. We pleaded for God's mercy. In his sovereignty, he chose not to answer our prayers exactly as we wanted. But God sustained us through that ordeal. He is God and we are not. This is a fallen world where death is real and bad things happen. When we pray, we must leave the outcome up to God, trusting that he will use each situation for his ultimate glory and our ultimate good.

Not all Habits Are Bad

Another aspect of prayer that Daniel modeled for us is that he made it a regular habit. He didn't pray only when in crisis. Prayer was part of his daily routine. I've heard it said that for the believer, Bible study and prayer are like inhaling and exhaling. If we don't do those two things, we are depleting ourselves spiritually, making it more difficult to move forward through the trials and struggles of life.

In Daniel chapter 6, the prophet modeled the practice of regular prayer. He was so consistent in this discipline that his enemies counted on it. If you'll recall from our study of chapter 6, Daniel's habit of daily prayer is what led to his unplanned tour of the lions' den. Three times per day he set aside for prayer. Let's look at the section of Daniel chapter 6 that details this for us.

> These administrators and satraps went as a group to the king and said: "May King Darius live forever! The royal administrators, prefects, satraps, advisers and governors have all agreed that the king should issue an edict and enforce the decree that anyone who prays to any god or human being during the next thirty days, except to you, Your Majesty, shall be thrown into the lions' den. Now, Your Majesty, issue the decree and put it in writing so that it cannot be altered—in accordance with the law of the Medes and Persians, which cannot be repealed." So King Darius put the decree in writing.
>
> Now when Daniel learned that the decree had been published, he went home to his upstairs room where the windows opened toward Jerusalem. Three times a day he got down on his knees and prayed, giving thanks to his God, just as he had done before. Then these men went as a group and found Daniel praying and

asking God for help. So they went to the king and spoke to him about his royal decree: "Did you not publish a decree that during the next thirty days anyone who prays to any god or human being except to you, Your Majesty, would be thrown into the lions' den?" (Daniel 6:6-12).

Take notice of a few things about Daniel's model of prayer that we find in this passage. He had a humble posture, a thankful attitude, and a specific ask.

The prophet was on his knees praying. Often our posture can lead our heart. There's something about raising hands in praise of God, bending our knees in humility toward God, or lifting our gaze in awe of God that leads us emotionally into God's presence. It also signals our humility to our Creator and Savior.

Daniel had a thankful attitude, purposefully thanking God for (and perhaps reminding himself of) all the blessings God had provided. Psalm 100:4 reminds us, "Enter his gates with thanksgiving and his courts with praise; give thanks to him and praise his name." We need never forget that God is holy. He's not our equal, or our buddy. He is almighty God. Yes, he is also our loving and tender heavenly Father—but he is utterly holy, perfect, and omnipotent! He has blessed us beyond what we could ever pay back. He gave his sinless Son so that we might be made right with God through Christ. May we never forget!

Finally, after entering into God's presence through a posture of humility and an attitude of thankfulness, Daniel brings his immediate needs before the Lord. Once again, Daniel risked it all on his Lord. The prophet continued his practice of prayer knowing it would lead to the lions' den. While in prayer he brought his need to the Lord. He implored the Lord to intervene. He didn't know how the Lord would do it. He didn't know if the Lord would do it. But he simply brought the need to the Lord and then he let God be God.

Surely Daniel prayed that God would keep him out of the lions' den. If so, then we know that God said "no" to that request. But God wasn't done there. God answered Daniel in an unexpected way—by shutting the mouths of the lions. God will often answer prayer in different ways than we expect so that he gets greater glory and we experience more growth!

As we pray and trust God, the fact that our rescue is not a guaranteed outcome is what makes our faith more real. Bad things do often happen to good people. But God is still God. Daniel's three friends didn't know if they were going to survive the fiery furnace of Daniel chapter 3, but they stood their ground anyway.

In the book of Job, this man who had lost his health, wealth, family, and dignity was able to say, "Though he slay me, yet will I hope in him" (Job 13:15).

Getting More Than We Bargained For

Sometimes when God's people seek him intensely, they get more than they bargained for. There have been a few intersections in my life—moments of crisis or struggle—when I have spent more intense times of prayer with the Lord. I hate to admit it, but my prayers are much more fervent in times of struggle than in times of blessing. We tend to take God for granted when things are going well. Often, he will allow struggles to come our way to cause us to draw closer to him. I can honestly say I have grown much more through struggle than through blessing.

During these few intense seasons of prayer and seeking, God has often given me more than I bargained for. In hindsight, these seasons have proven to be the most pivotal, game-changing moments of my life. I didn't see it during the trial, but looking back, it is clear that God was changing my trajectory.

Daniel chapter 9 opens with the prophet wondering about Jeremiah's prediction that God's people would return to Jerusalem after 70 years of captivity. The time was up, and the prospect seemed impossible to Daniel. His heartfelt grief over Israel's guilt and acknowledgment of God's faithfulness led him to seek God through intense prayer. The greater the prayer need, the more intense the time of seeking becomes.

Let's take a look at a few verses from Daniel's prayer in Daniel 9:1-19. Notice the increased level of detail, humility, confession, and intentionality in the description below. It's a long section (19 verses) so I recommend you pause here and read it in its entirety. I've chosen a few select verses below to point out a few observations.

In Daniel 9:1-4, we read:

> In the first year of Darius son of Xerxes (a Mede by descent), who was made ruler over the Babylonian kingdom—in the first year of his reign, I, Daniel, understood from the Scriptures, according to the word of the Lord given to Jeremiah the prophet, that the desolation of Jerusalem would last seventy years. So I turned to the Lord God and pleaded with him in prayer and petition, in fasting, and in sackcloth and ashes.
>
> I prayed to the Lord my God and confessed.

Notice again that Daniel pleads with the Lord. Only God can move the dial on seemingly impossible situations. Next, notice he mentions "prayer and petition." He was bringing a specific need to the Lord. Also, notice this time he was going without food and he took the posture and attitude of mourning for something that had been lost. The prophet took physical actions that connected to the spiritual reality.

We must remember that though we are physical and material—made up of flesh and bone—our bodies were created by God to serve him, and our physical nature connects to the spiritual reality.

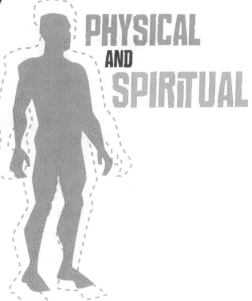

That is one reason sexual immorality is so harmful to human beings. It is also why, here in this passage, Daniel clearly understood the connection between our physical bodies and connecting with the Creator through humble prayer.

Next, the prophet spends 11 verses (4-14) confessing his sins and the sins of his people to the Lord. The Abrahamic and Davidic covenants found in Genesis 12 and 2 Samuel 7 respectively, were unconditional covenants between

God and the Jewish people. But the Mosaic covenant was conditional, based on obedience to God while in the promised land. A careful study of Daniel's confessional recap in verses 4-14 lines up with the curses for breaking the Mosaic covenant that God laid out in Deuteronomy 28. This description of blessings and curses based on the behavior of God's people proved to be prophetic. Everything God said would happen came to pass, and Daniel acknowledges that here in this section of his prayer.

Following Daniel's Deuteronomy 28 confessional recap, the prophet then turns his words to reminding God of how he came through for Daniel's people in the past. He appeals to God's character to petition on behalf of his people to receive God's mercy and grace. Finally, he reminds God that his glory is attached to Jerusalem and the Jewish people. Ponder those components as you read the following passage, which completes Daniel's prayer:

> Now, Lord our God, who brought your people out of Egypt with a mighty hand and who made for yourself a name that endures to this day, we have sinned, we have done wrong. Lord, in keeping with all your righteous acts, turn away your anger and your wrath from Jerusalem, your city, your holy hill. Our sins and the iniquities of our ancestors have made Jerusalem and your people an object of scorn to all those around us.
>
> Now, our God, hear the prayers and petitions of your servant. For your sake, Lord, look with favor on your desolate sanctuary. Give ear, our God, and hear; open your eyes and see the desolation of the city that bears your Name. We do not make requests of you because we are righteous, but because of your great mercy. Lord, listen! Lord, forgive! Lord, hear and act! For your sake, my God, do not delay, because your city and your people bear your Name (Daniel 9:15-19).

Now here's the kicker: Daniel was praying for one thing—the return of his people to Jerusalem—but God gave him so much more. In response to this humble prayer from the prophet, God not only made a way for the prophesied return to occur, but he also gave Daniel a prophecy covering Jewish history from Daniel's time to the end of time! Daniel asked for clarity on 70

490 YEARS

70 YEARS

years, and God gave him a prophecy that was seven times 70 years. This has to do with the 70-weeks prophecy in Daniel 9, which we covered in detail in chapter 13.

When we seek God humbly and with the right motives, we just might get more than we bargained for. God is looking for those who are submitted to him. There is a lot of kingdom work yet to be done, and the main ability God is looking for among people is availability.

Setting Ourselves Aside

The final key passage that displays Daniel's prayer life is found in the lead-in to Daniel's final vision. In Daniel 10:1-6, we read:

> In the third year of Cyrus king of Persia, a revelation was given to Daniel (who was called Belteshazzar). Its message was true and it concerned a great war. The understanding of the message came to him in a vision.
>
> At that time I, Daniel, mourned for three weeks. I ate no choice food; no meat or wine touched my lips; and I used no lotions at all until the three weeks were over.
>
> On the twenty-fourth day of the first month, as I was standing on the bank of the great river, the Tigris, I looked up and there before me was a man dressed in linen, with a belt of fine gold from Uphaz

around his waist. His body was like topaz, his face like lightning, his eyes like flaming torches, his arms and legs like the gleam of burnished bronze, and his voice like the sound of a multitude.

Remember, this was what led to the long, drawn-out introduction to the vision contained in Daniel 11–12. Daniel began fasting early in the month and fasted for 21 days. On the twenty-fourth day, he received the prophetic vision. If he began his fast on day one of the first month, then God allowed for a three-day gap between the end of the prayer and the giving of the vision.

In chapter 10 of this book, I pointed out the timing of this intense season of prayer. We're not told why Daniel was fasting, but this would have been after his people had been allowed (by decree of King Cyrus, as prophesied in Isaiah 44–45) to return to their homeland. The prophet likely heard about the struggles to rebuild as reports came in about how Ezra and Nehemiah faced challenges there. The text tells us Daniel was mourning, so whatever the issue was, it laid heavily on his heart. As usual, Daniel had a deep passion for his people to honor the Lord and for God's will to be done. So much so, that he was willing to go without in order to make his prayers as effective as possible.

It doesn't seem that Daniel went without food completely. He limited his eating to only plain food—just the basics. Perhaps it was another vegetable diet, as we witnessed in Daniel chapter 1. That appears to be the case, as the text mentions that the prophet didn't eat any meat or drink any wine. He also used no lotions. He let his appearance speak to the fact that he was setting aside this time to seek the Lord.

Shedding Light on Prayer from the New Testament

Trying to face our challenges without prayer is like trying to drive a car without gasoline or trying to scuba dive without an oxygen tank. It is make or break. It is that important.

Those of us who have received Christ can go directly to God. We don't need a priest or a mediator. The cross cut out the middleman. We now have direct access to the throne of grace (Hebrews 4:16). As believers in Jesus Christ, the Bible informs us that we are chosen, royal priests. Peter tells us, "You are a chosen people, a royal priesthood, a holy nation, God's special possession, that you may declare the praises of him who called you out of darkness into his wonderful light" (1 Peter 2:9).

At times, we take it for granted what a privilege it is to be able to pray directly to the Creator of all things. He has demonstrated his compassionate love for us by sending his only Son to die for us on the cross.

Unlike the lowercase-*g* gods of other religions, the one true God is a deeply personal being who offers eternal life and longs to maintain an intimate, ever-deepening relationship with his children.

On occasion, this may cause us to forget that we must also approach him with great reverence and respect. In addition to boldly approaching God's throne of grace, Scripture also reminds us to have a reverent, respectful fear of God. Not the kind of fear that awaits a terrible fate, but instead a deep awe and respect for the righteous character and might of the Creator.

Here are a few more verses from the New Testament that you may want to consider:

> Philippians 4:6-7—"Do not be anxious about anything, but in every situation, by prayer and petition, with thanksgiving, present your requests to God. And the peace of God, which transcends all understanding, will guard your hearts and your minds in Christ Jesus."

> 1 John 5:14—"This is the confidence we have in approaching God: that if we ask anything according to his will, he hears us."

> James 4:2-3—"You desire but do not have, so you kill. You covet but you cannot get what you want, so you quarrel and fight. You do not have because you do not ask God. When you ask, you do not receive, because you ask with wrong motives, that you may spend what you get on your pleasures."

Thankfully, God made a way through the cross. Grace is God's unmerited favor offered to those who put their trust in Christ. God is not a puzzle to be unlocked; he is a safe place to collapse into, a shelter in the storm, and a Father to run to. We can come boldly to him through what Christ accomplished on the cross!

Putting It All into Practice

I'll confess that far too often, I try to manage life using my own strength. Then, usually after struggling for a while on my own, at some point it hits me that I need to go to the Savior. Why is it that so often, prayer is our last resort instead of our first? We must resist living like prayer agnostics and start leaning in to the practice—especially in the days in which we live!

At the time of writing this, the congregation at my church is about to enter an annual time of corporate prayer and fasting. For 30 days in the month of September, we are challenged to fast in some way as we seek the Lord and ask for his favor and direction.

When it comes to prayer, you don't have to be legalistic about it. Don't get bogged down in formulas. Sometimes we can make coming to God in prayer much more complex than it needs to be. The important things are: intentionality, regularity, and having the right motives. Exactly how you pray is up to you.

The various attributes distilled from Daniel's example give us plenty of practical ways to deepen our own prayer life. As you read through this chapter, what were some things that jumped out at you? What are some specific steps you think the Lord may be leading you to implement next in your life? Write those down and set some specific prayer goals with dates attached to them. It's been said that 100 percent of goals that are not set are never reached. Take some time and write down your prayer goals in the graphic below.

CHAPTER 18

Dare to Be a Daniel

Your eyes saw my unformed body; all the days ordained for me were written in your book before one of them came to be.

PSALM 139:16

As you can see, Daniel is an amazing book on both a practical level as well as a prophetic/historical level. Chiefly, it foretells the key events of the time of the end. No wonder the prophets longed to see our day! Jesus informed his disciples that "many prophets and righteous people longed to see what you see but did not see it, and to hear what you hear but did not hear it" (Matthew 13:17).

The prophets longed to see the arrival of the Messiah and the restoration of all things. We are privileged to be able to see—in hindsight—the fulfillment of prophecies related to the first coming of the Messiah. We're also the first generation in almost 2,000 years who has seen prophecy fulfilled with the rebirth of Israel and its continual growth (in terms of population, financial strength, and military might). And we are witnessing key stage-setting events taking place in preparation for future prophecies to be fulfilled.

At the same time, we're witnessing the decline of morality, the increase of wickedness and violence, and the growing pagan influence of the occult and other surprising influences. This paradox is exactly what we should expect to see in the last days as we draw closer to the return of Christ.

BIBLE PROPHECY WILL BLOW YOUR MIND!

Therefore, we have a golden opportunity to point people to Christ and his gospel. Though it feels like most won't listen, we must dare to be a Daniel and resist the pull of culture and the draw of hopelessness. Lights shine brightest when the world is at its darkest. We must rise to the occasion and dare to be a Daniel—to live godly lives in the face of growing evil. We must be willing to preach the gospel even when we feel like Noah or Jeremiah who preached their entire lifetimes with seemingly little result.

What's Next?

If you'll recall the beginning of our journey together, I highlighted the sovereignty of God over the kingdoms of men and how Daniel was written during the darkest of times. Here we are again—to varying degrees around the globe—caught in the current of darkening days. Yet God is still sovereign.

Prophetically speaking, we know that the next event set to occur is the rapture of the church. As I've highlighted in this book, the stage is so clearly being set for the future tribulation period that will take place after the rapture. Therefore, we can conclude that the rapture may be closer than many Christians realize. Perhaps it will occur in our lifetime. Take a look at today's newsfeed. Can you imagine what it will show in five years? In ten years? Everything we're witnessing today serves as metaphorical lights on the dashboard, making us aware to the earth's final act.

How bad will it get prior to the rapture? That we do not know. It does appear to me, as I study Scripture, that global financial collapse, global war, and global famine will not occur until after the rapture and the start of the tribulation period. The first four seal judgments detail the rise of antichrist, global war, global famine, and global plague. In any case, the more time that passes, the worse it is going to get. As a friend of mine often says, "Normal isn't coming back, but Jesus is!"

As the Judeo-Christian principles in America and the West continue to erode and weaken, there may come a time when some of us have to take a courageous stand. Depending on our careers, spheres of influence, leadership roles, or public visibility, we may be forced to do so. Like Shadrach, Meshach, and Abednego in the ordeal of the fiery furnace, they weren't looking for a fight but it came to them.

In the cases of Nebuchadnezzar's order to kill all wise men of Babylon, the fiery furnace, and the lions' den, God chose to protect the lives of his faithful followers. But anyone who has studied the topic of Christian persecution knows this is not always the case. The brutal martyrdom of Coptic Christians filmed on the shores of Libya at the hand of ISIS members in 2015 serves as a recent reminder that Christian martyrdom still occurs.

Various ministries that track and catalog Christian persecution around the world, such as Open Doors or The Voice of the Martyrs, regularly report the sobering statistics. The Open Doors *World Watch List 2023*[17] showed that in just the previous year there had been:

- Over 360 million Christians living in places where they experience high levels of persecution and discrimination.
- 5,621 Christians killed for their faith.
- 2,110 churches and other Christian buildings attacked.
- 4,542 believers detained without trial, arrested, sentenced, or imprisoned.

Even right here in America, soft persecution is growing. What I mean by soft is that believers are not giving up their lives on a regular basis, but they are giving up careers, losing opportunities, being cancelled on social media, and experiencing other forms of oppression.

It is possible that this will get worse. If nothing else, it will cause further division unless there is another great awakening prior to the Lord's return.

In Hebrews chapter 11—known as the faith hall of fame—we read a recap of some of the giants of the faith from the Old Testament. The first 34 verses name several Old Testament heroes and how God miraculously protected them. Verse 34 even alludes to the account of the fiery furnace from the book of Daniel.

But then we encounter a few verses that are a bit more sobering. They demonstrate that sometimes God allows his own to become the victims of martyrdom. We read this in verses 35-39:

> There were others who were tortured, refusing to be released so that they might gain an even better resurrection. Some faced jeers

and flogging, and even chains and imprisonment. They were put to death by stoning; they were sawed in two; they were killed by the sword. They went about in sheepskins and goatskins, destitute, persecuted and mistreated—the world was not worthy of them. They wandered in deserts and mountains, living in caves and in holes in the ground.

CAN YOU JUST READ THE FIRST PART OF HEBREWS 11 PLEASE?

These were all commended for their faith, yet none of them received what had been promised.

Perhaps we need to take a lesson from the pages of Scripture and the lives of these bold martyrs. We may never be called to lay down our lives for the sake of the gospel, but perhaps we'll be called to make some uncomfortable stands. Perhaps our faith will cost us something. In any case, we need to adopt a willingness to die trying. When we die to ourselves daily, then we can really begin to live. In a short measure of time on the grand scale of things, at the end of our lives we will all be either in the presence of the Lord (if we know him as Savior) or separated from the Lord, tragically awaiting the final judgment described at the end of the book of Revelation (20:11-15).

TIME FLIES

As the world becomes increasingly unhinged, let us shift our focus and our efforts to eternal matters. Let's set our minds on things above (Colossians 3:2) and store up treasures in heaven (Matthew 6:19-20), where there will be no instability, uncertainty, or loss—ever. Though we don't look for it, let us be prepared to face the lions' dens of the day with courage and an unwavering integrity as God continues to construct our character with rebar for such a time as this as we await the rapture of the church.

Dare to Be a Daniel—Now More Than Ever

Will you dare to be a Daniel? In whatever platform you have, will you make a commitment to walk by faith and not by sight? Will you lean in to God's sovereign design for your life and the times in which he has placed you?

Now more than ever, we need to…

- choose to be wholly dedicated to the Lord no matter what comes our way.
- form or maintain a habit of prayer.
- seek him more deeply through fasting and intentional times of prayer.
- remember fulfilled prophecy.
- have confidence that all end-times prophecies will also be fulfilled literally.
- realize it is possible we are very near their fulfillment.

Daniel and his three friends were remnant believers. They did not witness the wide-scale acceptance of the one true God. But they lived faithfully anyway. We are remnant believers, living in the waning moments of the church age.

In Luke 18:8, Jesus asked the rhetorical question, "When the Son of Man comes, will he find faith on the earth?" In 2 Thessalonians 2:3, Paul states that a massive falling away from the faith must occur before the tribulation begins. These and several other passages paint the clear picture that at the time of the end, true biblical Christianity will be diminishing. But there will always be a remnant.

Here are some verses to keep close to our hearts and minds as the world grows darker and as we dare to be Daniels—living as remnant believers:

> Romans 8:18—"I consider that our present sufferings are not worth comparing with the glory that will be revealed in us."
>
> 1 Corinthians 2:9—"'What no eye has seen, what no ear has heard, and what no human mind has conceived'—the things God has prepared for those who love him."
>
> 2 Timothy 4:7-8—"I have fought the good fight, I have finished the race, I have kept the faith. Now there is in store for me the crown of righteousness, which the Lord, the righteous Judge, will award to me on that day—and not only to me, but also to all who have longed for his appearing."

Finally, here's one more verse that provides specific end-times marching orders. In Hebrews 10:23-25, we're challenged with these words:

> Let us hold unswervingly to the hope we profess, for he who promised is faithful. And let us consider how we may spur one another on toward love and good deeds, not giving up meeting together, as some are in the habit of doing, but encouraging one another—and all the more as you see the Day approaching.

Scripture is clear that we can see the Day of the Lord (the tribulation period and the return of Christ) approaching—and we do! Hold unswervingly to your faith. Challenge believers to do great things in these last days. Don't stop going to church. Encourage other believers—all the more as you see the Day approaching!

Be a strong Christian. Be prepared for whatever may lie ahead, trusting in God's sovereign care. We look back at an empty tomb; we look up to an occupied throne; and we look forward to a victorious future that is already settled in heaven. When we anchor our thoughts and emotions to those key facts, we can still thrive as believers, no matter what we may face in this life. Dare to be a Daniel. Normal isn't coming back…but Jesus is!

NOTES

1. Kenneth G. Hanna, *From Moses to Malachi: Exploring the Old Testament* (Bloomington, IN: CrossBooks, 2014), 405.

2. John F. Walvoord, *Daniel*, The John Walvoord Prophecy Commentaries, eds. Charles H. Dyer and Philip E. Rawley (Chicago: Moody Publishers, 2012), 141.

3. Thomas L. Constable, *Notes on Daniel Commentary* (March 2022), 99, at https://planobiblechapel.org/tcon/notes/pdf/daniel.pdf.

4. Herodotus, *The Landmark Herodotus—The Histories*, ed. Robert B. Strassler, trans. Andrea L. Purvis (New York: Pantheon Books, Random House, 2007), 1.178-1.181.

5. John F. Walvoord, *Daniel: The Key to Prophetic Revelation* (Chicago: Moody Press, 1971), 147.

6. A.T. Olmstead, *History of the Persian Empire* (Chicago: University of Chicago Press, 1948), 50.

7. Charles Lee Feinberg, *Daniel: The Kingdom of the Lord* (Winona Lake, IN: BMH Books, 1981), 65-66.

8. Elvina M. Hall, "Jesus Paid It All," 1865.

9. Reuters Graphics, "Earthquake in Haiti," *Reuters Graphics* (August 17, 2021), at https://graphics.reuters.com/HAITI-QUAKE/DAMAGE/lbvgnnnjnpq/.

10. History.com Editors, "Massive Earthquake Strikes Haiti," *History*, A&E Television Networks (January 18, 2022), at https://www.history.com/this-day-in-history/massive-earthquake-strikes-haiti.

11. "The History of Rebar Concrete Construction," *GRA-Gulf Coast Construction, LLC* (blog), (March 3, 2015), at https://gra-gcc.com/blog/the-history-of-rebar-concrete-construction/.

12. Flavius Josephus. *The Works of Josephus*. Translated by William Whiston. (London: T. Nelson and Sons, 1866; reprint ed. Peabody, MA.: Hendrickson Publishers, 1988), *Antiquities of the Jews, Book 10, chap. 10, sec. 4.*

13. Flavius Josephus. *The Works of Josephus*. Translated by William Whiston. (London: T. Nelson and Sons, 1866; reprint ed. Peabody, MA.: Hendrickson Publishers, 1988), *Antiquities of the Jews, Book 11, chap. 8, sec. 5.*

14. Dates and details adapted from: John F. Walvoord, *Daniel*, Walvoord Commentaries, 322–346.

15. Polybius, *The Histories*, ed. Brian McGing, trans. Robin Waterfield (New York: Oxford University Press, 2010), 5.86.5

16. See, for example, Harold W. Hoehner, *Chronological Aspects of the Life of Christ* (Grand Rapids, MI: Zondervan, 1977), 138; *The Bible Knowledge Commentary: Old Testament*, gen. eds. John F. Walvoord and Roy B. Zuck (Colorado Springs, CO: David C. Cook, 1985), 1363; and Tim LaHaye and Thomas Ice, *Charting the End Times* (Eugene, OR: Harvest House, 2001, 2021), 89.

17. "World Watch List 2023," *Open Doors* (2023), at https://www.opendoors.org/en-US/persecution/countries/. Note: When accessing this site, the data displayed on this page will reflect the current year's report of statistics.

Other Great Reading by Todd Hampson

The Non-Prophet's Guide™ to the End Times

Do you tend to avoid studying books of the Bible like Revelation and Ezekiel? Does it feel like words such as *rapture* and *apocalypse* fly right over your head? It's common to dismiss these and other topics related to Bible prophecy as irrelevant and…well…too complicated.

But God's Word says, "Blessed is the one who reads aloud the words of this prophecy, and blessed are those who hear it and take to heart what is written in it, because the time is near" (Revelation 1:3).

Prepare to be blessed in a meaningful way! *The Non-Prophet's Guide™ to the End Times* combines engaging illustrations with down-to-earth explanations to help you navigate the ins and outs of Bible prophecy. There's no better time to grasp God's plans for the future—and for you—than this very moment.

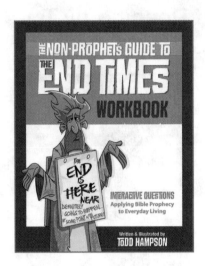

The Non-Prophet's Guide™ to the End Times Workbook

Dig deeper into what the Bible says about the end times and gain insight into God's plan for your future. Todd Hampson's companion workbook to his best-selling *The Non-Prophet's Guide™ to the End Times* makes the challenging study of Bible prophecy clear, understandable, and fun.

With more than 100 helpful and humorous graphics and illustrations, you can explore scriptural prophecies and discover answers for your questions about the last days, such as...

- How does fulfilled Bible prophecy affect our view of prophecies not yet fulfilled?

- What can we learn from those who were watching at Jesus's first coming?

- How can we discern between conspiracy theories and trustworthy facts that line up with end-time geopolitical signs?

The Non-Prophet's Guide™ to the Book of Revelation

If the final book of the Bible has ever left you scratching your head or wondering what to make of plagues and horsemen, your friendly Non-Prophet is here to help you read Revelation as never before.

Full of engaging graphics, author and illustrator Todd Hampson has created a user-friendly guide to John's prophecies about the last days. This concise and appealing study

- removes the fear factor and demystifies the capstone book of the Bible
- provides biblical clarity about the key events in the end-times
- helps reclaim your hope, confidence, and joy in the promised future

The Non-Prophet's Guide™ to the Book of Revelation offers informative study tools for understanding its prophecies, and practical challenges to apply God's truths to your life today.

The Non-Prophet's Guide™ to Spiritual Warfare

Even as a Christian, it can be difficult to discern the facts about the supernatural nature of good and evil. How much has pop culture influenced our ideas about angels and demons? Why do we as Christians face spiritual warfare when the Holy Spirit dwells within us? What limits exist on Satan's powers?

In *The Non-Prophet's Guide™ to Spiritual Warfare*, bestselling author and illustrator Todd Hampson gets to the heart of your questions about spiritual battles, angels, demons, the nature of evil, and more. With Todd's signature combination of light-hearted illustrations and thoughtful applications of Scripture, this guide is both easy to understand and deeply informative.

You will learn to...

- discern between cultural myths and biblical facts about the supernatural
- recognize the real threats you face while remaining grounded in God's truth
- understand why being ready to stand against demonic influence is more important now than ever before

The Non-Prophet's Guide™ to Spiritual Warfare will give you the resources you need to champion spiritual battles, while inspiring you to dive deeper into God's Word to equip yourself with truth.

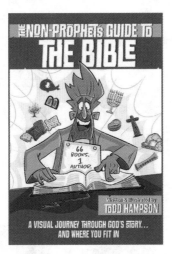

The Non-Prophet's Guide™ to the Bible

The world's all-time bestseller, the Bible is truly unique: an ancient collection of 66 separate books written across 1,500 years that fits together like a perfectly crafted puzzle. It proclaims itself to be the Word of God—and supports this claim with hundreds of specific, now-fulfilled prophecies.

Because of its massive cultural impact, readers of all backgrounds and beliefs ask questions about the Bible's context, history, purpose, and reliability. Enter *The Non-Prophet's Guide™ to the Bible*: a bright, infographic-packed panorama designed to give you

- a section-by-section overview of the Bible, illuminating each book's distinct role in telling God's story

- a crash course on who wrote the Scriptures, when they were written, and how they were preserved through the ages

- the compelling case for why you can believe the Bible truly is the Word of God

Whether you're a longtime believer looking to better understand Scripture or an interested newcomer seeking answers about Christianity, this accessible guide provides the insight and information you need to see how the Bible portrays a global history that has unfolded in the direction of God's promises.

The Chronological Guide to Bible Prophecy

This fun and informative book provides a comprehensive survey of the many prophecies found in Scripture, underlining their themes and illuminating why they bring us hope today. This resource will deepen your sense of wonder for the Bible's accuracy, while guiding you through a timeline of God's pledges to his people. You will...

- examine completed Bible prophecies—and witness how these unbroken promises create clear and compelling apologetics for your faith

- understand the prophesied events that are still to come and the order in which they will occur

- grow in reverence for our incredible God, who uses prophecy to make his amazing faithfulness known to us

To learn more about our Harvest Prophecy resources, please visit:

www.HarvestProphecyHQ.com

HARVEST PROPHECY
AN IMPRINT OF HARVEST HOUSE PUBLISHERS